LOVE
POEMS

a lifetime of poems
for the love
of my life

ROLAND PEASLEE

BALBOA.
PRESS

A DIVISION OF HAY HOUSE

Balboa Press books may be ordered through booksellers or by contacting:

Balboa Press
A Division of Hay House
1663 Liberty Drive
Bloomington, IN 47403
www.balboapress.com
1 (877) 407-4847

Print information available on the last page.

ISBN: 978-1-9822-2681-7 (sc)
ISBN: 978-1-9822-2682-4 (e)

Balboa Press rev. date: 8/6/2019

Roland Peaslee first met the love of his life Bonnie Rehder, in October 1958. For weeks, Roland's friend, Jon Klover, tried to get them together by saying "You must meet my girl's best friend." And finally, they did, in the hospital cafeteria at 06:00 hours on a Saturday morning. Three weeks later Roland left Fort Sam Houston, San Antonio, Texas for Korea.

In November 1959, Roland arrived back in the USA after spending 13 months in the combat zone at the 121st Evac Hospital often mentioned in the TV series M*A*S*H. The journey home in an old DC 7-B was harrowing, but waiting to surprise him at Orland CA, was Bonnie.

Their correspondence courtship ended when Bonnie had her Fort Ord orders changed to Fort Hood, Texas. There Roland was Chief of the Eye Clinic. They were married April 2nd 1960.

These poems comprise recollections of Roland and Bonnie's life together. Married for almost 6 decades; Bonnie was the loving mother of Alan (March 1962); Brian (June 1964), Jay (March 1967), and Dian (December 1968).

Our children encouraged me to have the collection published and what a gift Reid Tracy has provided with printing and binding our remembrances. Thank you, Reid!

R.G.P. March 2019

BONNIE PEASLEE

ANNIVERSARY

There is no way for me to say
That "this day" has seemed more gay—
Than the first with you
For joy has grown the whole year through.

With the joys we've known,
Our love has grown.
Dreams and schemes lovingly sown
Building a palace without malice—

Time plus love; Oh, who can measure—
Joy and tears, pain and pleasure?
Time has brought us ANNIVERSARY.
With love, I give you special "versery."

Your Roland

April 2, 1961, Our First Anniversary

For Bonnie,

For all the moments that we
   share,
I daily find a need for prayer.
The joys we find both night
   and day
Are sweeter still because
   you say—
   "I love you."

Your Roland
3/24/61

Dear Bonnie,

Thank you for your love
and the National Geographic Traveler
and your love and kisses
and the new atlas
and your love, kisses and understanding
and the chocolate cashews
and your love and kisses
and understanding and
warm caring
and the safety helmet
and your love, kisses,
understanding, warm
caring and mothering,
and chocolate covered orange
peel and hazelnut chocolate
and your love, kisses, understanding
and warm caring
and mothering
and for the accordion lamp.

all my love,
Roland, the
"Husbunny"

With a bit of rime,
There comes a time
When the word, "wife"
Means all of one man's life.

This is what you mean
        to me
As round the hands go.
Reminding me in all I see
That you are my ego.

Love Roland
April 2 1965

Dear Dian:

You were determined!
You ran the race!
Your key was courage
And you kept the pace.

Only in doing can we succeed;
By using reserved strength
You conquered the speed
Which brought you through

To claim third place!

CONGRATULATIONS!!!

With so much love,
Your grandmother.

Dorothy Peaslee

Hershey National Track Meet 1978

TRIBUTE TO BARBARA
July 1, 1995

Through lenses thick, thin and remodeling din,
We had our "SUPER BARB"
Who directed our patients in.
From building blue to building brown,
Barb never did let us down.
From building brown to building red,
She made sure we stayed ahead.

Through changing Medicare and Medicaid
Barb was there for the whole parade.
No matter that numerous changes persisted,
Barb never came at us double-fisted.
Though at times we surely did perturb her,
There was never lightning and thunder.

Though the years saw office tasks multiplying,
Barb would guide with hustle undying.
While doctors were determining twenty-twenty,
Barb regulated the paperwork aplenty.
When computer woes came and caused a fuss,
Barb learned to guide, sort and discuss.

Time is measured by a clock
Whether for office or athletic jock.
But now Barb will have less pressing affairs.
She can look at the clock and say "WHO CARES?"

Our hands and hearts are joined in saying;
We were so much better for your staying!

Roland G. Peaslee, O.D.
June 30, 1995

Dearest Bonnie,

We're in this love together
SUN, WIND, RAIN—WHATEVER.
So, it's onward we travel,
We'll not see our love unravel.

Some say love is blind
But that is so unkind.
For us, as fates entwine
We'll not feel the knot unwind.

Seen thru the eyes of love,
With blessings from above
We'll see the gold and silver sheen
Of a dream unlike we've yet seen—

Valentine's Day, 2005

TO BONNIE
03-25-05

As your birthday does appear
I hope you'll always know dear
You are loved! Oh, so sincere!

Amid those times of darkest night
When dreams put up a fight,
Try with all your might—
TO HOLD ON TIGHT!

Almost forty-five years and holding firm—
Let's move beyond to re-affirm,
Our one true love is here to stay
Only til forever, plus a day—

Love, Roland

As our love arrives on April
>   SECOND,
It causes me to sincerely
>   RECKON
That through the years we've
>   TENDED
Our marriage, like music
>   BLENDED.
We await more years to yet
>   UNFOLD,
And so our covenant becomes
>   THE MOLD.
From fifty-eight in San Antone,
When we'd said "I'm ALONE,"
To fifty-nine at an airport
>   GATE
Was when we foresaw our
>   FUTURE MATE.

(3 PM, APRIL SECOND, 1960)

As you see me arrive, call me Roland Rimer,
My tumbling words possess a timer.
Mimes Portnoy their message, though paid no wages
Using postures, they write their pages.
By my thoughts condensed are given to a refiner,
To create the ultimate multi-liner.

What say it better—songs, words or a letter?
It's always my goal to express it better—
The constant goal of my created verses
Will never be treasure placed in purses.

The image of a symphony plays in my mind
With instruments of varied kind;
All in concert—projecting and perfecting.
Led by a skilled director, the music becomes a rector.
Blending all the skills combined
Thus it is delivered to us, quite refined.

Bonnie gives love to me in a symphonic basket.
My joy is complete in the receiving—
A BLESSING, NEVER LEAVING!

Roland

For you I could some cookies bake
    Or some gadget I could make.
But all of those have left me cold,
Because they will have never told—
How your love, my greatest win,
Is what your love for me Has been—

      Roland, your
      Husbunny

THE TRUE HEART

Whenever I hear the topic, heart
My mind always gives a start—
to travel back for these many a year—
to savor the joy of having you near.

Some people's hearts show wear and tear
That often strips emotions bare.
But you have been my guide oh so far,
To show your love without a scar.

Love,
Roland

(2005)

ODE TO A POTTY SEAT

Sit high on your throne, potty chair
We hail you, from your perch up there—

May you in your duty never fail—
May you always have tinkling in your pail!

We welcome you among us boys
For you we'll even leave our toys.

And so as you begin life's spin,
May you and Mommy always win.

2005 or 2006 to Dian

I love you, BONNIE

Happy Valentine's Day

♥ A TRIBUTE

As years travel by, in my minds' eye,
There is always YOU;
Daily making joys accrue.

Your presence is a special git.
It always grants me a lift.

When two hearts beat as one
Together seeking the horizon;
A valentine is only paper.
BUT—YOU and I are each
          others' best favor!

2006

I can only give you love that lasts forever:
COUNTRY WALKS IN SPRINGTIME
HANDS TO HOLD WHEN LEAVES BEGIN TO FALL
A COZY HOUSE—
WARM FOR A WINTER'S NIGHT AND MORE.
ALL I'M ASKING IN RETURN IS—SAY IT'S ME
YOU PLAN FOR, <u>NOW</u> AND <u>EVERMORE</u>.

Valentine's Day, 2007

The beating heart within me
    still singing
The treasured sound of your voice.
    OR
Sighting you ahead in the mall
Let's me fondly think and recall —
The moments of tenderness and
    nights of joy,
A treasure of pleasure.

For me it's been a simple route—
Loving you day in, day out,
    (but with <u>never</u> a doubt)—
Rain or shine, needing you
    all the while, with your
    caring style.
For I'm your man for all time;
It is enough that you are
    MINE.

Lovingly,
Roland

MEMORIES

How can there be sweeter
      memories for thee and me—1968
Such as Fort Som and Corpus Christi?
Island sand and shells galore
Found as we explored the shore.
Coconuts and water sports,
Together we saw them thereabouts.

Love, like the ever-moving tides,
Came to use and still abides.
Winters, summers, falls and springs
All have come on the seasons' wings.

We always knew our bond was
      more than the rings—
Our love is written on our heartstrings.

          Love,
          Roland

August 2007

"YOU"

From Korea, it became
        life anew, because of <u>YOU</u>.
What a change, not to see
        Life as a constant zoo.

With <u>you</u> as my guide,
        a comfort by my side;
It became a lifetimes'
        ride—

With no reason to hide,
We came.
We loved.
We tried and thus
        we still abide—

_____   _____   _____

No matter what I do,
My minds' eye will
Always see <u>YOU</u>!

Love,
Roland
12/12/07

FOR MY VALENTINE, 2008

See us as the sun peeks through
With leafless trees playing peek-a-boo.
Soon there will be squirrel gymnastics
Arriving for their breakfast fix.
These feeders are for the birds you know.
Never mind—they come and go.

And here we are encountering LIFE,
Threading our paths avoiding strife.
We drift along using uncertain wings;
Seeking refuge from happenings
     That drive us into the rocks—
     Placing us in a box.
So we scurry out before it docks
While hearing the clock that ticks and tocks.

The steady anchor swimming intact
Is our abiding love, our VALENTINE PACT.
There we find, beside and above,
Our ever-present treasure of
     LOVE,
     FOREVER YOURS,
     Roland

For Your Collection

From time to time I receive letters from people and I try to include them when I have the room. The following came from one of our builders and I hope you

<u>Enjoy</u>

A MISSION BUILDER CREDO

So you want to build your church
and not be told, "you're in a lurch."
There is one group not to be denied,
They will abide and turn the tide.

Mission Builders to the tasking!
Not in the sun will they be basking.
Tell people they perform Mission Builder work
As long as someone makes the coffee perk.

And if someone asks what they'll tackle
Answer, "walls, floor, roof, and spackle."
There's the job; there'll be no shirking,
When they arrive prepared for working.

Living in their mobile vehicles
They'll save that church some precious nickles
And when you hear the noisy pounding,
you'll be certain they are founding
A parish home for folks abounding.

As work is done for the living King
And some fingers get a hammering;
You'll be assured there is no hiding
Of their faith beneath the siding.

Thanks to Roland Peaslee 03/08

TO IRENE

Gymnastics skills come to Irene,
Perhaps it's what keeps her lean.
(But studies do have to intervene.)
Now she'll have to face a test,
Where other YOUTH will do their best;
And tally facts will not be guessed.

In the meantime studies loom
And so she's running to her room.
Doing homework oh so clever
May keep her from the dishwasher lever.

Wisconsin looms—Hello SHEBOYGAN!
Here I come to my toboggan;
I'm ready to participate.
Daddy, please don't be late!

by Grandpa Peaslee
03-23-08

Ode to Frank & Kent

Here a cheer for Frank & Kent
Busy with their books unbent,
Seeking out the facts that matter
There's no time for pitter-patter.

But when it comes to basketball
Thru the hoops the ball must fall.
Be sure you are ready to calculate
All their scores, early and late;
Then add the totals for each date.

Let's hold the group from Royal Oak
For they bring smiles to all their folk.
But now's the time for a shower soak.

Grandpa Peaslee
03/23/08

Ode to a Birthday:

As on we go—How do we know
If our trail will end, or become a bend?
We're like a searching hound
Never knowing what may be found.

There is no magic telescope,
We raise our sights, and also HOPE
That our lives will find a helpful nope;
Because life is not always clean.
It may be mean, lean or in-between.

We're told the Ancients believed in FATE,
But it's not for us to sit and wait.
We prepare our hooks and fix the bait,
Then out we change through the swinging gate.

Hold the KARMA! We'll cause life to change
And declare worthwhile (with a smile)
That we have made a pile.
Then we'll retire, prepare to gauge
Whether we've acquired gold—or sausage.

(Be advised not to watch the making of sausage.)

Let me tell you how I fell,
(you'll hear no bell.)
There was no searching or sudden lurching,
Looking high and wide on every side.

You come to me just like the creeping tide.
And made me say, "Here I'll stay!"—
            Forever and a day.
Not for a thrill or a test of will;
You're my love—my heart you fill—

Love, Roland

May 2008

Mother's Day declares we can be sentimental
Buying petals, "SAY IT WITH FLOWERS."
But we so lack the wished-for powers,
To deliver love crowned with rainbow showers.

Over the years now forty and eight;
I hope it's never to late to initiate
And say, "I LOVE YOU" to my soul mate.

There is a reward for each other's believing
As we blended our lives, a created weaving.
See the tapestry we shone, no ordinary pleasure.
Hard to measure—It's our love-treasure.

Love, Roland

Nothing else reminds us like beach front waves
Of what a '58 memory saves.
> The wind, sand and fun on Mustang
> Far away from any gang.
The 7 to 7 ferry that we rode—
Then we drove back to Ft. Sam, our abode.

The time we spent exploring sea and sand,
> plus shelling—hand-in-hand
Was the kindling of a growing flame
That we did not wish to tame.
Our deepening love found it was no game;
We found a treasure in each other's name.

Our kiss refreshes (and revives our lives)
Like releasing a thousand bee hives,
Forming the honeycomb of our lives—
Whenever we stand hand-in-hand,
We're forever linked by our wedding band
Silver circles tell us tales
Of dreams and love that never fails.

We journeyed our separate paths—alone—
Til at least love's seeds were sown.
Or paths were crossed and blended,
> quite unintended,
Creating a lover's tale
Assisted by the U.S. Mail

'58 was the date, that became our fate.
It was an opening gate—
When we found a mate.
Time flies on by with details blended,
And we persist on our path unended.

We declare our love shows no desire
For us to say "IT'S TIME TO RETIRE."
Now we cheer the year that is so dear,
We show no fear as we onward peer.
Father Time marcheson so steady,
And we reply "READY FREDDY."

With all my love,
Roland

Here's a call for Reunion of the REHDERS!
No need to bring pails, lures, or waders
There may be fish shown on the menu,
Plus lots of other foods offered to you.

There'll be no hushing of the discussing
With brothers, sisters and cousins and gushing;
The pictures will be vivid mixtures.
Together again there's a tune finding
That as before there's binding and re-winding.
Is there a measure of this pleasure?

There has to be some compelling for re-telling
Why Vern would say, "3 day visits are swell,
Since at 3 days fish begin to smell,"
Grandpa's sentences were presented
        (with certainty intended).
Wasted words could not be found
In any chat with Vern around.
Fern was always cooking and cheerful
And who hasn't heard, "Just one more spoonful!"

And then always trying to remember
When we had the worst December!
We'll all have to be on-the-ball
So we can places and names recall.
Frightful and delightful spans go by, my oh my,
But in five years we'll all sigh—
When do we again say "bye bye"?
Every five years, hear the cheers!

1ST ED.
Behold the campaign, off and running
With lots of verbiage and always cunning.
Let's not talk Whitewater or malfeasance,
It interrupts the TV AD-DANCE.
Monica is off-limits; so is FARRAKAN.
Beware the media, filtering all it can!

How about personal freedom versus mandates
Let's have TAX FACTS and sound estimates,
(Plus how tax rates affect stalemates!)
Some candidates care not what they demonize—
Just whatever they can GULLIBULLIZE.'
Swallow at your peril—
Whatever comes from the democrat barrel.

2ND ED.
Methinks that there will never be
A democrat without a taxing fee—
        (Even if they say "IT'S FREE").
Because whenever there are public monies
Democrats rush out, shouting funnies.
TAX AND SPEND is their normal manner
Hear the clamor! Wave their banner!
There is a side bar on their menu;
It's a mandate: "We're good for you!"

Hear their cry: "SOAK THE RICH!"
Beating drums to sell their pitch.
There'll be special classes, as time passes—
  (to decrease terror to the wearer).
Should you choose to wear their cloak,
You'll discover it's a joke!
FOR NOW YOU HOLD A PIG IN A POKE.

Whether you find these words amusing
  (or too bruising)—
Be assured of just one thing
If democrats win this fling,
There'll be no hiding from their deciding.

This would be all so funny
Were it not for the plight of our money.
Enuf already?

JAY'S PARADE

There'll be a time, none to compare
When all your thoughts will make you dare
To assemble a plan somewhat startling.
There'll be starting, daring and then departing
There are ideas just waiting to go,
And then it's time to start the show.

There'll be no details you can delete
With all the countless forms to complete
(Feel the heat, deadlines to beat).
And now the facts all seem to meet
In a presentation sweet and neat.
Now there's no room for a retreat.

There will be questions you can bet
But "What you see is what you get."
The plans are drawn extremely straight.
Will you wait or participate?
There will be chasing of ideas hot
(And other ingredients mix in the pot)
Now let us view just what we've got.

There are some ideas not quite pure—
Just label me an entrepreneur!

(about 2000)

"49 and Counting"

It's very true, our love came to us fresh and new.
The event surpassing; and oh, so neat—a joyous treat...
Now we've travelled beyond the familiar
And the totals have become above par.

There have been paths that uncovered pain.
There've been some days that came with rain.
But we also slowed for views of beauty
While performing our tasks of duty.

Your poet sees candles lit, and then recalls
Events that came a-blending in our love;
                mending and attendings—
We know love's benefit; the lives we knit;
For as the candles dim, then fade,
We can recall how plans were made and
                those bills were paid—
But our promises were not mislaid.
We kept our vows, faithful and true
So thus our love could daily re-new—

The world shows wonderful things to do,
But only becomes memorable with <u>YOU</u>.
Until your poet runs out of rime.
I'll love you for all time—

April 02, 2009

California, Here I Come!

California gold once caused a rush,
But now gold is in the fields, green and lush
Almonds, plums, lettuce and rice—
Plenty of flavors—strawberries so nice—

The beaches beckon surfers so tanned.
They bring their boards, all waxed by hand.
Ignoring small waves, only huge will do.
The ocean delivers them quite a few.
Let me look. This one's for you!

The palm trees sway and promise dates,
But only for those who seek water and wait.
The snow-capped peaks promise an evening breeze
Will cool the desert floor, there to please.
The shifting plates squeeze and seize, the tremors tease.

Hollywood creates a scene complete with stars;
Costumes a-glitter, plus bars and cars.
Here the dreamers must finally awaken
                (done with fakin')
Their tally taken and finally shaken—
Horace Greely said, "GO WEST YOUNG MAN!"
California says, "Come see us if you can."
From beach to mountain and desert sand.
Your trip will surely leave you tanned

RGP
03/23/09

32

Mother's Day, 2009

Home again to sow and mow,
Bean pots seeded and flowers weeded,
Asparagus thriving and dandelions conniving—
With no end to their yellowness aspiring.
Now, with Mother's Day arriving,
There's another day for thanking you for all you do—
(more than a few);
Because you keep us thriving.
On the road or at the desk
Swatting away at the bookwork pest,
I am so proud that you've allowed
Our lives to be blessed with pleasantness.
Please know my happiness is fully confessed.

Roland

San Antonio Anniversary

There is never a precise August date
That signals meeting you, my treasured mate.
We found a Texas beat, with no retreat.
From a joining of emotion, we required no other potion.

Now fifty years later, with more mileage on our meter,
We look back to review how we began in a Ford two seater,
Finding we <u>still</u> drive a "two door Ford."
The coupe that roared has led us toward
Added mileage that appears to be—
Around the bend for you and me.

Love, Roland
August, 2008

(In memory of our first meeting)

(The Motor Home with two doors)

Whenever our wheels are rolling Texas-bound
I'll always remember the Iowa Girl I found.
Not a Yellow Rose of Texas
      (near the Alamo)
She was from Ioway, I'll have you know!
At Fort Sam Houston in middle August
      (summer uniforms a must)—
Our paths blended as summer ended;
Then flying the PACIFIC, not so terrific.

Letters were sent forth and back
And you even sent me a "cake-pack."
It's fifty years since we re-united
And then wedding vows were recited.
The two door FORD was a '51—
And we drove it with some fun.
The OLDS come along in sixty-four
And it was also just a two door.

The pick-up camper in '67 was the beginning
Of travels we're still envisioning.
For me you are a dream come true.
Your love unfolding is my fuel.
For you are my life-long renewal.

Love, Roland

08/09/09

TEXAS gave us historical momentos—
Ft. Sam Houston, Ft. Hood and San Jacinto.
50 years to and fro and on we go,
Travelling still, time passed so fast.

From pickup camper and motorhomes we've been on the go—
Coast to coast, borders found now we know.
Our eyes have seen a scenic feast great to least
Mountains & oceans, cities that thrive;
FILL'ER UP, we're ready to drive.

Louisville Hickory & Grapevine too
Northlake and the Milwaukee Zoo.
We've seen the sights old and new.
At Houston's Main Street and the Lakeview,
Off to Nova Scotia, Newfoundland too
We've stayed at quite a few—Clark's Summit with
          lightning strikes & parked below New Orlean's dikes
Washington snows came at Lynden town—
We never let it keep us down—Two dollar Tuesdays
          there we found.
Casino milk machine slots made lots of sound
As their silly cows become unwound.

Perhaps there's still a beach we'll find, with palm trees lined.
Sampling sun in FLORDIA LAND will find us tanned,
Where shells are washed by sea and sand.
There we'll stroll, hand-in-hand.

          By R G Peaslee

FOR DAUGHTER DIAN
(12-03-09)

You were our December surprise in '68.
Arriving late, choosing your own date,
With fingernails long but oh so dainty
My clippers were a first priority—
That year you were under our Christmas tree, for all to see.

All the events we've enjoyed recalling
As you caused records to be falling,
Like the impossible A in Drivers Ed
Became another high as you moved ahead.

The calendar pages say you've reached forty-one;
And that means another year has begun.
Facing familiar routines that must be won
Hopefully there will also be fun—

So we now enter the autumn of our years,
Once again sending our love so it appears
To tell you '68 remains unique for us—
Woven into our lives you're wondrous—

YOUR DAD

Be prepared for your JOURNEY to BOURNE!
Mission Builders gather and unite.
It's time to hike with all your might,
And soon Bourne will be in sight.

You know drills, saws and hammering,
Now there's time to start the yammering.
There'll be food and fun and stories galore,
Be sure you're there to add some more—

Texas BBQ is on the menu
Plus other items sure to please you.
The choice to come is clear—
So gather round from far and near.

No candy I've found is ever sweet as you,
And through all our years, this will be true.
Whether it's summer or fall, winter or springs
You remain my queen—see our rings?
Our years have become more woven and entwined,
Ever stronger, a bond that will not unwind.

Now this "HEART'S DAY" welcomes Russell Stover.
Will anyone say giving candy is over?
Back to the first line of this verse;
Can a test for sweetness be perverse?
Now and a kiss and test the candy.
Hopefully you'll find that it's just dandy!

As Our Golden We Are Beholden'
(3/3/2010)

Day-by-day, I'm more in love with you; and
You need to know—
There is no end to my devotion; deeper than the ocean.
With each years turnings, your love still gives me yearning

Seeing you gives me the same heart thrill
As with your Oakland, CA, arrival still.
Then the tears at Temple, Texas,
      with my leaving you behind—
Our future yet to unwind.
Your love would not hide or be denied.
Many dreams have become true
And always—only—because of you.

Texas travels are trips we re-trace
And nothing will erase
The first trip to that Padre Shore,
We could later repeat with two little boys.
How our love had grown, able to soar—ever more.

As we renew with old friends, lover,
We find our trips are not yet over.
The motorhome still fits in our plans—
Holding hands; with mops, cans and pans.

I love being here with you
As we reach the warm
Gold of our Sept. years
Soft summer breezes
Flow thru the trees—
A touch of your gentleness
And rest assured as
Years go by with you
By my side—you
Always preside over
My heart—

Roland, Still in Love
March 2010

DIAN'S 50TH POEM

Goodness gracious—how can it be?
Mom and Dad have been married forty-seven plus three!

Wasn't it just yesterday they met in Armyland?
I am certain that Dad was so handsome in uniform and tanned.
Dad was "taken" by thin dietician.
Did she know she would be in for so much fun?

Four kids would follow in a quick six years.
Can you imagine the stress and maybe a few tears?
Very few in Fairfield could boast: three boys and a girl.
They must have been a happy family—for sure!

The oldest would follow like Dad to Knox.
For he is an eye doctor and smart as a fox.
Next came the engineer and father to FIVE!
Can you imagine how busy it is in their Detroit HIVE?

The lure of the mountains would call the next son in line.
Designing, insurance, and banking suit his fancy just fine.
"No snow for me" said the daughter who's last.
"I'll take care of patients and get them out the door fast."

Mom and Dad, Thanks for all you have done.
You made growing up in a house with values and virtues fun!

And so we congratulate them—
would you raise your glass with me?
We wish them well and another fifty!

With All My Love,
Daughter Dian

(AT OUR FIFTIETH ANNIVERSARY – 2010, April 2nd)

The Voyages
(April 2010)

How will I count the ways I love you?
My wife, my friend and navigator too.
We've been on lots of trips we two
Visiting places and faces, quite a few.

As we see the roads unwind
NOT knowing what we'll find
Our love is always on my mind,
A treasure exceeding any measure.

As we journey to places yet unseen
We'll always keep our senses keen—
For detours that might be mean
Bumps and nuts are there to be found
Traveling routes that we've unwound.

Gatlinburg honeymoon, then a quaint little village
Perched on a rocky hillage,
Finding Cade's Cove from a by-gone day,
People doing things in an older way.

Padre island's "NORTHER" and Arkansas "FIVE"
White River ferry with a grain truck on board
Kept us from being bored.
There was Crater lake and Going to the Sun
Mt. Rainier and down the coast for Disney fun.
(Discerning Dean would be added to our fun.)

Myrtle Beach, Ft. Myers and Key West
New York, D.C., Nova Scotia—Which is best?
Sheep River Canyon was another event
(with an axle bent)
FLIN FLON and North Star Lake
Kananaskis trail, a unique route to take.

North to Alaska, little gold we found
But miles and miles were then unwound.
Copper Harbor and thimble berry pie to bake
Coho salmon and sailing on Superior Lake.
Rathbun, Sarah and Lake Shetek
Where bullheads were landed by the peck.

So fifty years of travel have gone by—
        Let's give a sigh—
Yet knowing there'll be some roads yet to try.

RGP

It's so easy to remember, impossible to forget
All the tender moments we have met;
They make memories return alive
As we cruise through all our decades five.

I want all my tomorrows spent close to you;
And I'd like them to be better than new.
I'll let our embrace confess, we found happiness.
When dreams drift before you
Let all these tomorrows bring promise anew
To declare we're bound in love, "WE TWO."

Time spent kissing makes for reminiscing—
With sunrises, noontimes or setting sun;
You remain my <u>exclusive</u> one.
TENDER • THOUGHTFUL • TRUE • SINCERE
You remain to me always—in ALL ways
     NEAR & DEAR—

RGP

DAY IN—DAY OUT

The thoughts of you follow me about.
Morning, noon, twilight or night
These pleasant memories appear in rhyme,
Re-appearing and distilled by time.
We create pictures with no words, like a mime.

Our travels have driven us far and wide—
The label of "gypsy" has been applied,
We're still ready with maps to fold
Searching for new memories to hold.
Canyons, lakes and views we can't ignore,
Searching out more, opening another new door.

RGP Mother's Day
05-09-10

TO OUR DIAN
(June 2010)

FAST on the track and FAST in my heart
With my daily start, your picture sees me depart.
There's so many events to recall
How do I begin to name them all?

You were our grand surprise!
We placed you under the Christmas tree that year
And three little brothers were there to cheer—

That was 1968, but at the age of four
200 Highland was our home no more.
Off to 505 with lots more room
And no more Highland cars there to zoom.

Chasing your brothers out the front door
You knocked out a tooth at the age of four.
Putting it back was the best choice
So you would not have a lispy voice.

There were dancing, piano, basketball & track
Cross country and baseball—you had the knack.
To play first base with no errors at all
Was another record you did make
And always left runners in your wake
Your 800 record stood many a year
Til the Kuiken twin did appear—

So off to Luther with your Cordoba car,
A working summer in Colorado far.
Then nursing courses piled on high
Leading to Mayo's for a year
To master the floor skills without fear.

With lots of miles as a traveling nurse
Finding some duties, good bad and worse.
In Denton your masters' cape we came to see
Gold threads to show straight A's, "golly gee"!
Then claims work (on the road)
Caused you to master a new case load.

Now Timberidge is your place to be,
As your twins challenge you to see
What will be their next new feat
In their daily learnings they will complete.

Dad
06/05/10

48

THANKS FOR THE MEMORIES
(For our 50th Anniversary Party 2010)

Whole milk, not skim soft and sweet,
Nickel Hershey bars, were a treat.
Butter—Oh so soft and mellow,
Who had heard of the cholesterol fellow?
Nothing was "little," it was sugar & Karo
And no one had a diet with choices narrow.

Three gallons of gas for a buck
And here's a gift for good luck.
Plus windshields washed clean of muck.
Rockefellers and Phillips could only extort
Thirty-nine cents for oil, per quart.

Quarter pounder with shake and fries
That was ninety-nine cents for gals or guys
Brought to your car on roller skates
When the car hops scanned the lucky dates.

Here we are, sixty years later
With burger specials on the menu.
A dollar for a few bites of beef
And one thirty-nine for the glass of coke,
          What a joke!!

Nine ninety-five bought you specs at Bard's.
If lucky, you could see past your cards.
Driver's ed in a fifty Ford
With column shifting, no one was bored.

So here we are—we're quite a show
      As on we go,
Here guys and a gal plus all the offspring
Look at those eyes a'twinkling—
While grandparent's eyes are wrinkling.

When we begin a reckoning
We see time ahead still beckoning.
Bonnie says, "We're a lucky couple."
Let's hope the arms and legs stay supple.

Love, Roland

"1960 PLUS 50"
(Christmas 2010)

Songs in the air with holiday music and food we share,
Reminds me again of your constant, loving care.
Being near you is still a joy, and also fun;
Recalling many things we've seen and done.

As we approach the winter solstice
We know the winds will bring a chilling kiss.
Two heart's warmth will keep us cozy with checks so rosy,
Steady, not off and on like the furnace,
Always sure and steady with no fuss.

Our first Christmas tree was cut from cedar branches,
Cranberries and popcorn the tree enhancing.
Your cooking skill with skillet & popcorn popper—
No fridge or stove, so there we were
With card table and chairs our first furniture.
Then walking a block to our garden, pulling a wagon.
Our first Christmas with rent, insurance and payments cured,
Left us with twenty dollars secured.

200 Highland, our first house, standing tall
Where Alan and Brian played "LOOK IN THE
            BOXES" as they would crawl.
Then came a room addition for Jay's arrival.
Three brothers were almost a church pew full.
Dian changed the mix and filled the '58 IMPERIAL

From '64 to '72 we were on the run
A pick up camper took us places with our "chillun."
Enter the jolly green machine, a motorhome willing
Far and wide, tide to tide, coast to coast.
Then off to Alaska, two months that were the most.

505 Fairway in '72, three months of fixing to do.
Patching, painting and adding some new;
Family room, sun porch and a motorhome barn too.
Plan and spend, lots to do; plus more miles, quite a few—

By '80 we saw colleges in view to the east
#2 went south, #3 went north, then #4 northeast.
Activity levels never ceased—

Now 50 years have rolled on by, passed so fast.
Now watching the grands collection of colleges seeking,
Futures unwinding, allowing no peeking.
Now we live at 506 with less to fix.
We look back as the dark makes its mix.
We see a fine mix of our "FANTASTICS."

Love, Roland, Christmas 2010

Fifty-Oners
(2011)

We are fifty-oners, ever living in county 51.
We've had good fun, hon; and that's no pun.
In '58 we were in Padre Island's sun—
As we began to date we found demonstrations
HOW FATE had no wait until love opened
   heart's anticipations—

Our gypsy genes soon were found
And so we toured the U.S.A. around.
As a family we toured through Canada
But never were we searching for a panda.
Alaska gave us marvelous sights to see

There are routes we've yet to travel
And so before TIME can make days worse,
We'll keep maps handy to rehearse.
There one attractions we've yet to behold,
"Keep movin' on as long as you can," we are told;
So we'll look for new routes to be unrolled.

Nothing can compete with our memories neat,
That we have found in both cold and heat.
Now we'll not hesitate, anticipate or set a date
When we'll be towed into PARK & ROCK mode.
FATHER TIME will be the referee who rules that code.
And so together, our love carries us on
   Down life's road—

With all my love, Roland—April 2, 2011

Mother to our children, and grandma too;
My tally places you among the few
Who did set an example true, for all our crew.
Always faithful and so true.

We're told we made it look easy,
But your steady guiding was there to be
Through all the fog—always clearly—
Sorting out—one not always leisurely
Displaying love for all to see.

We're now the fifty-ones with steady will,
Walking up beckoning yonder hill—
Finding futures yet to unfold,
And memories made there to behold.

No one else has known my heart—
Surely won and never to part.

Love,
Always—
Roland

Doctors may come and go,
Assistants stay whether high or low,
They're doing the paper work
That one dare not shirk.

Computer "driven," you say we are—
And yet you never travel very far.
Going desk to desk all day long
Using canned music for your marching song.

Insurance, Medicaid, and Medicare,
The alphabet soup causes us to wear.
A smile at all times, every day,
And thus we make hay and earn our PAY.

My best effort in 30 minutes—
R. G. Peaslee, O.D.

So We're Off to Howard Johnson's Coffee Club
Where you'll find it's no village pub.
There's coffee, cookies and some hubbub,
Where Mr. Prill has high hopes for singing harmoniously
But even if on bended knee (or with a fat fee)
There'll be no way to achieve it with this party.

Numbers come and numbers go—
Ranging from high to low.
But who's to discover that mystery number
Only Howard will know—

Whether you be Johnson, Kurka, Koontz or Hunt
You can be caught in Howard's number
Even the chief himself has been caught
        By his own choices
Then laughed at by many voices—

June 2011

To Bonnie

There will be no poem as precious as my Bonnie.
From Ft. Sam to Padre Island, with lots of sand,
We met and found love's sweet command,
Then took each other by the hand.
We came to a town as complete unknowns,
There to build our future from bare bones.

The faith we knew and with work to share
Give us new lives beyond compare,
Plus family we consider so rare.
Accepting events that sadden and gladden
We formed ways to bend and mend and on each other to depend.

Now in the autumn of the life we know
Our path is still ahead, unfolding.
With unknown events that may be molding
To reveal joys and memories worth holding.

TIME

First light reveals diamonds in the grass
And robins searching for a work to grasp.
Climatis blooming says spring is here
And tasty garden items now appear.

Pine cones drop without a sound
And cardinals roll them to see what's found.
Squirrels are busy going round and round
As though their tree could be unwound.

Next we'll head into summer sensations
Vacations and tasty picnic rations.
Campfires and s'mores with fire-baked pies once more
Sunburns and bruises will appear for sure.

When leaves begin their steady fall,
Then it's time to perform a recall.
Shovels, spuds and brooms go in the hall—
Knowing snow will be returning soon,
Brightened at night, whitened by the moon.

Some will stay—some will travel.
Some will continue to unravel—
Never able to release their hold
On objects or inventory to be sold.

06/17/11

Some homecoming tales seem bold (when told)
With memories dear that will not grow old.
They spring fresh from long-ago days—
With classmates we recall, then amazed.

Because TIME creates a masking haze of days
Our lives translate from a dictionary
Recalling events filling our Pictionary.
Those memories both sweet and fond,
Recall events that forged a bond—
Almost trivial at time, thoughts they may be,
We'll recall those deeds, where memory leads
And fondly relate how we did succeed.

Now some classmate stroll only in our memory lane,
And we reminisce hearing an old refrain.
Our returning is a churning of laughter and tears,
And through it all our memory hears
The voices of friends both far and near.

RGP, July 2011
Pekin Community High School (Illinois)
50th Reunion

Ode to Bonnie

In the still of the night, my thoughts drift to you
It makes me know my years only count
When I recall you and things we would do

Time flies and we talk how things used to be
In so many ways I try to see
The events that shaped up in this Fairfield town
I can only say—through it all—
I'll love you til the moon is upside down

So driven by the need to make it so,
I can only say, "I love you, sweet and low"

Love, Roland 07-20-11

(07/15/11)

On we rush, we rave and $ave,
Thinking that we'll be $afe in our cave,
There within, all $nug & warm
We'll e$cape from alarm$ and harm$.

Fight or flight, the ancient choice,
Leave$ u$ u$ing an uncertain voice.
$hall we compromi$e or face our dutie$?
$hall we $top the noi$e$ and park our booty.

We wi$h to $urvive with $tack$ of $tuff,
But father time $ays choo$e and pay our due$
The new$ doe$ confu$e our view$--
Blaming big bo$$e$ for our lo$$e$.
We mu$t endure (not able to $tay the way we were)
We'll $trive to be $ure and $ecure.
$houting loud in the circling crowd
We'll remain $teady, true and proud.

The world may pound and confound
But we'll not become unwound.
We'll $tay the cour$e, proud & un-bowed.
$teadfa$t with faith we declare $o hallowed.

Author's Note: The dollar ign are a reminder of motivation$
that are alway$ pre$ent, a $tumbling block for our goal$.

R. G. Peaslee

OUR JOURNEY

Days begin with you by my side
And as long as memories cling at all
I'll be remembering events big and small
Many things we've seen and done
While caring, sharing and having fun.

For all my tomorrows you've been the one,
Because you are my moon and sun—

Ft. Sam days, Padre Beach, trips to recall
Recollections with pictures in books or on the wall.
Offsprings four, then out the door,
Guiding lives with values never foreign
We filled daily pages morn by morn
Never to be discarded or even torn.

From the book of lives that were started
When your wedding veil was parted;
That kiss caused clouds to be lifted
For dreams emerging that were gifted.

July 23, 2011

To Bonnie:

There will never be another you,
Whether morning, noon or nighttime, too.
There's no other match mate that will do,
Making each passing day interesting and new.

Like rays from a diamond rare
Your refracted light is beyond compare.
Not visible with an ordinary lens
It takes "your man" who knows and sends
His love and devotion as he intends.

RGP
07/25/11

ODE TO GWEN

Gwen's coming! Dust be in fear!
There's no place to hide when Gwen is here.
Birthday, rain, hail or winds that blow
She'll be here, that we know.

Always smiling, thorough and sure—
She brings the cleaning cure,
No dirt will now endure
Against her cleaning adventure.

So here's to the one and only Gwen.
She's after any dirt that could offend.
We'll be sure to easily see
Her work has always earned her fee.

RGP 07/25/11

Love came around a dining hall corner
(Though I was unknowingly)
Going to be knocked off my tee.

I thought I was a free-wheeling ball,
NOT tethered or secured to any wall.
But there were lures by no design of yours;
That led me to treasure our time together
No matter any changes in the weather

We happily say that we are glad
Good days have outnumbered the bad.
But that only scratches the surface
Of all the events we can still discuss.

We now remind each other of names and faces
No longer on the tip of our tongue—
As they were when we were young.
Recalling faces and places our memory embraces;
We enjoy our recollections before the march of time erases
The best moments of all those unforgettable places and faces.

07/26/11

Rendevouz

And now we've made our poem rhyme.
We alone know how we met our time.
We're Iowa-born and bred, then Iowa-wed;
No one could predict how we'd be led.
With hearts warmed in Texas, then to Korea lifted
To a steel cot, poorly-fed and fun forfeited,
Then came Oakland, where we were reunited.

RGP 07/28/11

OUR MISSION

There's never been another one
Who determined our searching's done,
And finished because our hearts were won.

The years have numbered fifty-three
Will you agree they sure came rapidly?
From the summer of fifty-eight
Fate would not allow us to hesitate.

There were flights over oceans blue
And there were letters—quite a few.
Army orders made our lives conform
To decisions that became our norm.
Army life did have its day—
Before we could return to IOWAY.

Now we live in the autumn of our lives,
Our love continues and survives.
As love has led us and still abides
We count our blessings like ocean tides.
Supported by faith that onward guides
We trust beyond whatever the future hides.

RGP 08/11/11

The Windmills of My Mind

When my thinking is in cadence and rime,
Sometimes there arrives a lag in time
When the proper word will not beckon
The thought, pattern or word with which to reckon.
Time marches with an unending pace
         (pushing me with haste)
Searching for that lost thought now erased.

More searching often proves to be futile
For there is no opening that memory box
To find the key words freeing my mental locks.
Like a melody found I could only for a moment rent
Now I wish for its return—hear my lament.

Lastly because of the bind in my mind
I cannot chase, find or unwind
That word or phrase I should have underlined,
So then my poetic effort could then be signed.

RGP 08/11/11

"CUPID KNEW"

When February snows are falling
They say that's when CUPID comes calling.
But our CUPID came in summertime, so wise,
Quietly aiming, using a surprise disguise.
CUPID'S arrows flew without <u>logical</u> conclusion;
Forever with CUPID'S persuasion,
We might have said it was a passing illusion
CUPID knew in '58 that he would not wait
And leave us to still anticipate.

As our TEXAS TIME went all too fast
We acquired a pause—a time to wander
During my Korean Detour, a time to ponder.
Were "WE" to last as the months slid past?
Would we seek to become the other's responder?
Letters proved to bind us and we grew fonder.

I love your wisdom and compatibility
Though to count them would reach <u>infinity</u>.
You're the binding of our calendar's days
But not to be tallied along life's maze;
But each day is better because of my Bonnie's ways.

We're now near the door labelled fifty-four.
And there's never been a doubt arise
That you alone owned my heart from the very start.
Thus our CUPID, though in disguise, proved to be so very wise

Love, Roland, 2012

Christmas comes only once each year
But when you appear in any scene I'm near,
Time shortens because you brighten my year;
Always bringing love, great food and loving cheer.

We began with much love and little more.
We found our future was like an open door.
Sixteen months before our first house—and—
Then came a son who kept us on the run.

High chair, booster seat, car beds and such
Were in steady use as we kept in touch
With four heads, forty fingers and toes to match—
Plus appetites and activities of our busy bunch,
Our life was full of events we had to catch.

Now there is a red bud tree for you to see come spring.
We know not what will come as the birds return to sing
But please know you're my anchor and mainstay
Whether spring, summer, fall or a winter day.
FAITH, HOPE, AND LOVE are found in jewelry and poem;
And they're found whenever we roam
Because—you are the key to what makes our home.

Christmas Day fifty-two is underway
And come what may, no matter what I say,
For me, you're always the one that makes
Christmas bright and gay.

With love, always—
Roland

THE MAGIC KEY

All my best memories reveal <u>you</u> in the picture.
Countless recalls emerge from our mixture,
Our blended lives built with special architecture.
      (NOW—he assured)
The love we know in the central fixture.

We knew no recipe for the potion
That propelled our lives into motion.
Our balance sheet was labeled LOVE,
Composed with mutual emotion.

How will I relate our mutual goals
As we assumed our family's roles?
We entered life's gateway and paid our tolls,
Dealing with detours and troublesome holes;
And every step added to our memory bowls.
Life's path wove designs into our souls.

My thanks to you are far too few,
Your love penetrates me through and through.
Far beyond words or things you do,
<u>I can never write a poem as sweet as you!</u>

The SWEET-HEART label for you sings so true
Whenever my thoughts return to you.
Fortunate am I to be able to look back and see
How you added to life's pleasure
      (measure upon measure)
Whether it was work or leisure.

As March 25th creates #77, your magic key
There's only one place I choose to be;
Hand-in-hand under love's canopy.

All my love, Roland
March 25, 2012

BIRTH DAYS

Birthdays can be used to record a score
Whether in the air you soar
Or stroll the beach hearing the ocean's roar.
It is said they always go up, but never down—
A true tally on the road or stuck in town.
There's no change by wearing a new suit or gown.

One could say birthdays are life's measure
And no doubt are a record of grief and pleasure.
So what can be said in their defense?
Will your answer be non-committal.
          (or on-the fence)?
An inquiry of one's age may be shunned away
Because old memories remain filed in "past tense."

Do your memories return with quick recall?
Or do some stay hidden behind the mind's wall?
There are names lost in yesterday's hash
While others emerge like a photo flash.
Who was the funny guy we both recall
          (from a yesteryear)
Who made us laugh and then disappear?
Our heartthrobs' hand we loved to hold
Has become a memory cold when today re-told.

3/25/2012

HI BIRTHDAY GIRL,
Make the flags unfurl!
Call the salon for a cute new curl.
For Bonnie is like a precious pearl
Stand in line, let the spotlites whirl!

She's a daughter, sister and mother dear
Who brings a smile when you see her appear,
And then to all—becomes endeared.

Bonnie may—can—or will
Surpass any obstacle if someone's ill.
Gracious, dependable and thoughtful still,
She'll tackle those tasks that need fulfilled.

Any harsh words have never occurred
Rather she chooses to see events endured;
Her chosen action replacing a word
That was better left unheard.

Her husband adores her and calls her
            a treasure (beyond wordly measure).
Time after time her decisions prove wise
(though at that moment <u>un</u>recognized)—
But found later to be a worthy prize.

Love, Roland
3/25/12

Is poetry a literary measure
Of heartfelt words to describe one's pleasure
With people or events we wish to treasure.

No painting will ever capture the shore,
Because it is missing the tidal roar
No book can say it all, though huge or small.

A short sense of chosen rime
Forces us to choose, in a shortened time,
Words that describe and reach
      (and thus to teach)
Our favorite people far or near;
Who then can laugh—or—shed a tear—
Because the poet made "picture words" appear.

For Bonnie, April 2, 2012

Love, Roland

OUR ANNIVERSARY ONCE MORE

We can recall 1960 opened our future's door.
We heard familiar wedding vows from
        Years before—only—
This time we heard it was <u>US</u>, <u>forevermore</u>

The calendar proves we're at year fifty-two
And there were times when some events we knew
Played out "like a zoo."

But the rings we have worn on our fourth finger
Have bound each heart.
THUS ENTWINED—WE WOULD NEVER PART.

Love, Roland

4/2/12

PROGRESSION

In our lives, growing from two to six
The genes thus enriched, came to mix
Birthday candlesticks, halloween tricks
    and bikes to fix.

From babes in arm, then six to thirteen
The weeks flew by to signify (and dignify)
Progress made onwards to achievements high;
    that few could tie

The "Grands" stand poised and ready now
To begin their adventures and searching tours
Ready to tackle work and some leisures.
    —AND—
Hopeful one we that their faith endures.

Instead of "Mother, may I?" there emerges
"GOOD BYE," "FAREWELL" and we sigh,
Even as we know setting high and varied goals
Will certainly require payment of some tolls—

Roland 04-14-12

REMEMBERING APRIL
April 19, 2012

I'm sending a little bird to tell you how much I care
How much I miss you when we're not a pair.
When you appeared my heart grew aware
That without you, my life was so bare;
If not with you, my days were like being nowhere.

You've been able to make joys continue
So that each day love springs anew;
And each encounter we find and do
Makes time special for we two.

When seeing you come into view
It triggers my heart with love anew.
Hundreds of people have passed my view,
But I only have eyes for you.
All my "good tomorrows" belong with you.
The many trips, the laughs and good food too
Make all my dreams come true.

In every way on our lives' busy race
You captured my heart from place to place
You've made me wear more smiles
       lasting miles and miles.

Remembering April, when it all began
The day we said, "I DO" and "WE CAN";
Together we've kept love as our home base
As we've gone on our daily race, always
With hearts held in a firm embrace.

Our memories of events in the years we've had
Make me <u>REMEMBER</u> <u>APRIL</u>, and be glad.

Mother's Day is more than the hours twenty four.
It's a day that <u>should</u> include all 364.
Mother's Day is so much more than a phone call or flowers
For the hand that cradles a boy curled
Has the power to rock the world.

They say a baby changes everything—
For no one can predict what a baby will be bringing
The status quo goes a'whirling.

We'll hear it said from the offspring four
        (though they'll not be at the door)
"We're sending you our love for evermore."

Love's Day arrives with special meaning
Because of many events that came "in-betweening."
At times all these may produce some tears
When recalling many joys plus some fears.

Love, Roland May 13, 2012

They swim and win so well
Let's ring a bell!
It's the twins with double wins.
And they swim not using any fins.

Throw our daughter in the water
So she can catch them;
But they'll not let her near—
　　　　(HAVE NO FEAR)
Because they will swim with a faster gear.

Though not yet tall
There's a sign to be seen by all—
The silver medals on the wall.

Make noise for the Carmody boys,
For they can swim and win
With splashing noise!

By Grandpa Peaslee
07-29-12

There was a day in nineteen fifty-eight
That neither of us would anticipate.
Our meeting there led us to our lifemate.
It was our fate on that August date
To enter a gate we did not calculate.

We can look back when we became a pair—
In San Antonio, 4th Army HQ and
      the Quadrangle—still there.
Bill Abel's, Nighthawk café and the Red Barn
With its wall of neckties hanging on a strand of yarn.

We went to Padre and rode a small car ferry.
7AM to 7PM was its schedule, for that mile
So we did not linger or too long tarry.

Shells we collected are still displayed—
A parting gift that I had made,
Below a beach scene that does not fade.
Bound for Korea, a hardship tour,
We had that interval to endure, as it were;
Without predicting any of our future.

Oakland, CA, was a glad returning
With many thoughts that were churning.
Baby Carol Ann was in Bonnie's care
While Roland fixed supper with good menu fare.

From Los Alimitos to Dallas Naval Air
Hydraulic failure we had a scare to endure,
But we landed intact and secure.

On to Fort Hood to hospital and clinic.
Mononucleosis made Roland so sick,
    Which was no picnic.
Bonnie came to tell him (if entering) into hospital,
    "TELL YOUR WIFE!!"
Who shares your life.

From Texas to Iowa we did hasten,
Fairfield was our final destination.
Our family expanded and then disbanded,
As careers were pursued and jobs were landed.

So now we're in our retirement abode
When not motorhoming down the road.
We found our love when both were affected
    (and least expected).
We have our precious memories collected
Because our hearts were mutually selected.

Love, Roland
(Remembering 54 years)
Aug 2012

TO OUR FAIRFIELD THANKSGIVING
By GRANDPA

With Bonnie's several lists assisted,
our Thanksgiving feast will again be re-visited.
    With food and games, jokes and recollection,
    We'll once again be bound by affection—
    Derived from achievement and distinction.
    Our family has no roots in the mystical;
    Our re-told stories are historical, even at times, slightly rhetorical.
    But Thanksgiving is also logistical.
All the rolls, pies, cheesecake and such are not mystical to us at all.
    There's no escape from the mincemeat recipe
        (From before 1640).
    Those who relish the taste may not be a majority,
        But the taste is forever noteworthy.
Though our gathering may not be announced nationally
in tones CHURCHILLIAN,
    Our reunions have become memorable as one in a million.
    We are bound by stories most numerous,
    Some embellished to become humorous.
With time too short and miles to be travelled,
our recollections and memories will be unraveled.
    We are again united without stale mystery,
    We are proud and blessed with family history.
Though we have not amassed a family fortune,
we've striven to be steady—
    Whether at noon or under the moon.
As we now see genetics emerge that compose each person's tune,
    We cannot know if <u>OUR</u> farewells will be later or soon.
    We scripted your foundations not on a sand dune,
        But built on faith, hope and love,
    With the abiding gift from the past, beyond and above—

FOR BONNIE
CHRISTMAS 2012

I want you to <u>know</u> that I
    Love you more each
    Christmas than a year <u>ago</u>.

Christmas arrives each of day of
    The year when you appear.
    With your forgiving ways,
    You give my heart continued cheer.

Because you always give
    Much more than you receive,
    You've provided constant
    Joy with the events you weave.

As we once strung popcorn
    And cranberries our first year—
    Continuing along life's varied trails,
    Our love sustains us and never fails.

We still explore and record
    Life's events, as
    Measures of our pleasures.

We are blessed as we
    Recall memories
    from our marriage treasures.

Love always,
Roland

A TRIBUTE TO BONNIE

Even if clouds conceal the sun,
Your love shines readily and steadily,
Brightening the many places where we run.
It's your love I've found
Ever since you've been around.
Your love is so clear to me, whenever
    I find you near.

You locked up my dreaming.
For you were the dream-weaver that
    came to pass;
You were mine to love at last,
My heart became wrapped in 4 leaf clovers and
Rainbows appeared with no rain in the blue
And my love true grows <u>only</u> for you.

Our Texas meeting (somewhat fleeting) cemented
    our heart strings.
We began with strolls on an island beach
And our letters caused over extending.
Then you came re-uniting us in an
Oakland airport you were tending.

At age 25, you caused me to come alive.
You've become the sweetness in my cup.
Your affection creates love's confection
Sweeter than any other concoction.
Home is where you are, far or near.
At quarter til two, in the wee small
    hours of the morning

To touch you so slightly reminds me
of your love so sweet and tender, once
   again my dream-mender;
(the chef-in-charge of "soft and tender.")
The remembered tears at Temple, Texas,
Created a yearning for my returning to your embrace.
You're sweeter than any rose that grows
And I'm the one that <u>knows</u>.

You are the center of it all—
Whether spring, summer, winter or fall.
You're my shining star, day or night,
Always feeling it is so right.
My yearning was answered on the returning.

You're my <u>everything</u>, for sure
With no detours to endure.
Your arrival brought love so pure,
Not fickle or arbitrary.
Our romance caused us to marry—And—
Dian told us "we made it look so easy."
But our dreams never went astray.
Nothing to re-arrange; nothing to unwind,
We remain entwined.

Love, Roland

If I could present you with a mountain;
Then there would need to be a sparkling fountain.
It would be there, clearly showing
How refreshing <u>you</u> are for us, always knowing
Just what you always do with your loving ways
<u>Always</u> arranging mutually happy days.

Now—as we enter our autumn years
     (still shifting gears),
We seek new regions to discover what appears.
We knew <u>NOT</u> to call for a crystal ball.
That would surely bring fears and tears.
We are glad to walk hand-in-hand
And enjoyed our discovered views.
Those stay in our memory's treasures of our traveling pleasures.

We've seen mountains up close with glaciers frozen
And taken pictures with everyone posin'.
New friends we've found on those roads chosen,
And shared with them our memories of mountains,
     prairies and coastal oceans.

Valentine's Day, the annual "REFLECTION OF AFFECTION"
Reassures us both of our love's steady direction.
<u>FOR US </u>we've found life's special section—
Reserved for us with our partnership protection.

Love always, Husbunny Roland

NOON
02/14/13

I NEED TO TELL YOU AGAIN—TODAY—
   I <u>LOVE</u> YOU!
WHETHER CHEEK-TO-CHEEK OR A
WHISPER MEEK AND WEAK,
YOU'RE MY MAGNET, ANCHOR AND HOME BASE.

IT IS MY HOPE YOU FOUND
MY LOVE ALWAYS STEADY & PROFOUND,
ONLY FOR YOU—

Love, always,
Roland

THE MEASURE OF OUR TREASURE
(Feb 2013)

You are my anchor, my one and only.
Your steadiness sustains me—I'm never lonely.
You are the ultimate gift in my life,
You became my treasured WIFE.

Like a star, shining afar, you're my navigator
    (confronting an unknown path).
With a steady sprint turning me back,
    from events "down-turning,"
to continue the needed upward-yearning.

When you had to worry and endure '59 & '77,
While I did a lot of Rochesters Mayo walking,
My thoughts were recalling many events
That gave us pleasure when we did "re-talking."
In 2003, there would come another urgent surgical needs.

We know there are more crises likely to endure,
And we are not able to cancel or censure—
Yet they remain a mental weight in our leisure.

We hear the message from our heart of hearts.
We receive guidance from sources apart.
The gift of faith tells our inmost souls
That we must press onward with all life's goals
Relying on FAITH, life's "measure of treasure."

A TRIBUTE TO CASEY
(Feb 2013)

Now we hear voices blending
To his baton attending—
Collecting notes harmonious to a final ending,
We heard the sections carefully blending.

Music from history's library now fills the sanctuary,
Pleasing to our ear and summoning cheer—

We're here to state that music belongs
As a reminder to all listening throngs,
That when instruments and voices are aligned,
Wondrously heard and expertly combined,
The composition thus connected is a monument erected
To the soul of one who had skillfully directed.

Sincerely,
Roland

FOR YOU TO KNOW

Birthdays arrive with their fixed call
Whether the season is spring, summer or snowfall.
Now your date reads seventy-eight,
Another gate that would not wait.

So it's time to reiterate to my mate,
Never just insinuate or hesitate.
I must relate on this date
So you will surely know
That I have always loved you so!

There's been no end to that glow
That radiates tome as you come and go.
For me your smile overcomes my every low.

Rhyming words are my lame excuse,
With little time to lose, before a nite's snooze,
Discussing issues from life's zoos.
And even as we find clouds, snow or rain
As we journey along life's lane,
We reply "WE'RE GYPSIES" (to explain).

Forever as we travel to and fro
I must insure with affection pure
That you will always know
My love you never reaches "low"—

All my love, Husbunny Roland

March 25, 2013

We view the gulf and stuff
    we've seen before.
Recalling twenty years or more,
When we came to Ft. Myer's shore.
The dolphins perform and
    pelicans soar,
While parasailors try to go
    higher than before.

We're in the snow-free zone
Eating seafood with nary a bone.
The surf chases shore birds
    allowing no rest
As they run and search for
    their bug breakfast.

We're lucky we know, away
    from the snows.
We remember how pretty it
    is when the wind blows.

Now again, birthday time
    for Bonnie dear,
But no spanking will
    she fear,

Love, Roland

FAITH is a gift we are told
And as our path of life did unfold,
Our love arrived as a gift new and bold.
Now we enter the years called GOLD.

Looking back over the years now fifty-three,
    (As we sit and sip our tea)
We're aware that time has flown
Leaving memories tender, unique and ours alone.

There is no way for our clock to unwind
So our recollections become entwined,
Filling drawers one-by-one, in our mind,
While some faces and places remain behind.

It seemed our love came about rather fast,
Writing letters as a year went past.
My heart was placed into true love's clasp,
Embracing my heart and soul secure at last.

We have found and nurtured our true love,
    Becoming a father and a mother—
Never looking or seeking any other.
We were not driven with desire on fire,
We wanted love that led us to know
Gifts and blessings brought us to every
    new tomorrow.

I know no other choices or sources
    to replenish my spirits.
Your helpful presence gives constant benefits.
You own all my love with <u>no</u> limits.

Now hear me say, "I'll love you forever and a day!"
There are no reservations, come what may
As once again I say, "Happy Mother's Day."

Love always,
Roland

WE TEXAS TWO PLUS 55 YEARS
(Aug 26 2013)

There needs to be recognition of a grand event
That took place in TEXAS, so very important!

Boys meets girl while both march to Army intentions
Yet this was the time when love called
      "ATTENTION!"
Cupid's arrows (or the Holy Spirit) took quiet aim,
Causing a painless arrival with no headlines
      Or sudden fame—AND—
Nothing was ever the same.

As the calendar pages slid by one-by-one,
There were necessities of getting things done;
And we also found ways to have some fun.

There were times when rain fell on our parade;
And while needed changes were made,
Our loving hearts never strayed.

Now HEAR YE! HEAR YE!
Roland loves Bonnie, come and see!
And it's true forever and a day!

So I'll tell you in every way
My love is constant night and day.

Love, Roland
for our San Antonio, Texas, meeting date. August 1958

Tis the time of year to treasure again these we hold so dear.
They are a gift of time and devotion;
Giving of themselves with heart-felt emotion.
Bonnie, my love, does these actions with little fuss or commotion.

My years of life in your presence
Teaches me that my love for you never lessens.
You'll not be mentioned on World News Tonite
      (with a special feature sound bite)
Because their time slot is too short to recite
All the gifts and skills you've always brought
      every day and night.

This Christmas now is two thousand thirteen,
And we have been through many events in between.
Please know my love for you is ever so keen
For nothing ever reduces that love or can intervene.

YOU ARE THE GIFT TO MY LIFE, A LOVING WIFE.

Roland (Christmas 2012)

There is no Cupid hanging round our estate.
He flew away in '58, to seek other hearts on that date.

It's the best arrows he ever named
Finding us with those arrows he aimed.

As the miles go by, to places low and high,
We treasure Cupid's skill that found FT. SAM
      (without passing us by),
Before we became separated—one gal and one guy.

The RV Life has let us see more places than most,
With scenery and memories coast to coast.
All over Canada, from Texas, California and to the East
Our eyes and tummys have had a feast.

It's easy to say, "Let's go down the road—"
Let's find another place for our "RV abode."
We're still bound together, YOU and I;
And as we wander with TOM TOM's assistance,
We're ready to travel almost any distance.

Love, Roland

A Valentine Life

I'll have you know it's true,
I live to do things for you.
Your love has been a miraculous gift
And has always given me a special lift.

"Invictus" could have been my name
Being captain of my soul, as the goal,
Forever onward playing <u>MY</u> game.
It seemed to sound OK to be a loner
And never any reason to become a "poem donor."
There are songs written to celebrate love's call
And for love a man built the TAJ MAHAL.

Hopefully you'll discover a daily Valentine intended
To be a bridge from my heart,
Which you tenderly rescued and extended,

With our fulfillment attained with mutual care
We'll continue to be a VALENTINE PAIR.

Love always, Roland (2014)

OUR RV LIFE by RGP

We've stayed on the move to prove—
Moss never grows in tires kept on the move.
We've collected many miles of reflections
Absorbed while traveling in all four directions,
Oceans, lakes, redwood forest and prairies.
We've viewed steel mills, fishing boats and dairies.
To Alaska, Saskatchewan and Labrador,
                on Canada's coast,
We've been on countless roads and able to post
Memories and adventures. Raise a toast!

There have been flats, dead batteries and parts that fail;
And on Lake Superior we had no wind in our sail.
Alan and Dad paddled home to relate a sunburned tale.
South of FLIN FLON on NORTH STAR lake
We found lots of Northern Pike to take,
And mosquitos made us their prize.
Only their Alaskan cousins were larger,
              feasting on us to demonize.

We've been tanned on the sand; damp and wet—
And at times we've been towed.
But dried out, repaired and re-set
We rolled out again going down the road.

02/15/14

"WANDERLUSTER" by RGP
(March 2014)

"SNOW IS A NO-NO," when off to Florida we go,
Where we wander on the sands when tide is low
And warming breezes tease palm trees to and fro
This year will be about number THIRTY-FOUR by a shore,
Remember your sun screen, or you'll be sore.

We'll gaze across the bay to SANIBEL ISLE
And pay the toll to linger awhile.
While over there on Ding Darling's mile
We'll watch the alligators crawl their single file style.

Beaches are white with shells galore,
Now we see millions more, blown on shore.
Once we came after a hurricane's roar;
From regions remote they laid in the sun,
And our fun was finding the very unique one.

We've used a lot of gas to visit these beaches
Where snow and ice never reaches.
The seafood we find are tasty treats
Whether served to us along the streets—
OR, while we're seated on our balcony's seats.

Where will we be found, as we drive and wander yonder
We're seeking new color in sunsets to ponder.
We say, "We're gypsies off to find varied sights of any kind."
We'll enjoy the scenic roads, as they do unwind.

AT FORT MYERS BEACH
03/23/14

There'll come a time as we sit
Knowing the shrimp are waiting
For their boiling and butter basting—
While watching the people, dolphins and boats
Here on the beach where no one wears coats

Family and friends who've been a witness
      at this address
Have seen bungee-jumping and parasailing
While they rode a jet ski for wave-jumping.

It's miles of driving before arriving
In a semi-tropical scene, always striving,
To reward us for our escape,
From homes pummeled by wind and snow coming,
To freeze our bones (and cause a few moans)
As we commiserate on our phones.

Verbal sketching begins with my rhyming
    Time, thus conniving,
To capture phrases that continue their timely arriving—
To accept re-arrangement and thus ensure
A lodging in our memories, and so endure.
With critical removing, hopefully improving,
A poet's verse emerges to find a home secure.

The palm tree's branches tirelessly etch their sandy tracings
Knowing they must endure endless erasings,
Meanwhile the sun is ever stalking and
With a relentless surf desiring to moisten
The feet of people who are beach-walking—
Who try to remain above the high tides' balking
Relentlessly the waves resume their goal
    to mark high tide, but forced to recede
They retreat and slide back to the
    ocean where they hide.

We've secured our home's door latching
While we enjoy the warmth of sun's rays we're catching.
All too soon the calendar reads: "GO HOME!"
Thus ending our 35th Florida Roam
Those calendar numerals proclaim,
    with strict announcing
That we should again be homeward-bouncing.
Viewing the predictable calendar count
Forces us to assemble, pack and mount
Our horseless carriage for homeward jaunts,
Thus returning once more to our familiar haunts.

Your Travelling Lover,
Roland

102

P.S. I'm indebted to Ogden Nash
   Who showed poets how to serve verbal hash
   Connecting words with their rimes,
   To celebrate our special times.

OUR ESCAPE (March 2014)

There are times when simple words become slotted rimes,
And there's no urge to compose "verse perverse"
Here by an ocean beach where ice and snow will never reach
There's no windy wrath found along our path.

We're here to now measure our pleasure by spending our leisure
To again find seafood where we were
In an atmosphere along a seaside shore.

To sailors who now ready themselves to endure
          Their oceanic venture
Sail out towards their wind and water adventure
They're repeating one of men's ancient skills
To escape entrapment within shrouded hills
          from the drudgery of desks or mills.
So they'll require those calming pills.

As we unwind and find renewal by traveling far,
There's no urge to store views in a jar
Turning its sides to relive scenery afar.
Seeking in sights by day or by nites
Enlarges our memories of scenic delights.

We did not wait for our older days
To seek out those by-ways to view
Mountains & prairies or to gaze
Far into the oceans haze.

REFLECTIONS & DIRECTIONS
(2014)

When rain seeps and creeps through a leafy bower,
Seeds respond with their latent power,
To germinate and some to flower.
We observe this and receive assurance
Concerning our own earthly endurance.
We're building time capsules within our world
While events surround us and we are swirled.

The hidden traits of our past generations
Endow us with ever-emerging passions;
And unpredictable vexations
Can accompany our maturations.

At times unaware of how our heritage emerges
We fail to anticipate sudden urges
Driving us forward to explore
A world beyond our nearest door.

We're ready to find useful knowledge, and more,
To combine with the love that came before,
The ancestral drive to achieve and thus believe
There is a future domain for us to weave,
A future desire to conceive.

In Corinthians there's a verse that says,
"CONSISTENCY IS A JEWEL."
As our time moves forward with its daily accruals,
Our lines require refreshment & renewals.
But we have to know and control those
        urges that we find emerging
Detouring our best intentions because
        of unhealthy desires on other's urging.

The cost of integrity lost or broken
Is not just a fleeting token.
Our new persona has shown an altered presence—
Breaching a fence holding our best intents,
And our former allegiance now mends.

Roland G. Peaslee
03/25/14

When you speak low to me, there is further increase
In my love for you that I'll not release.
We two have found that potion with the label "RARE"
Now it's like a cloak that we wear,
Far beyond a couple's usual fare.

We are here to acknowledge we're one lucky pair
Enjoying our life's events together
Like the phrase "TWO BIRDS OF A FEATHER."

Life's perceiving gives meaning to the phrase
"TIME CANNOT ERASE THE WAYS THOSE
SPECIAL MOMENTS WE'VE EMBRACED."
We find them stored in our special memory's file case.

If one were to believe the tellers of fortune,
They would relate to you, "NO ONE IS IMMUNE
OR CAN DISMISS
Reponses to that one person's kiss,"
Which inspires and perpetuates our unique bliss.

Love,
Roland

I've never found any cause to pause
In my quest for the suitable clause—
That will express my renewal daily
By your love that binds and finds
My tributes to you, always come to mind.

Within your cloud of gentle affections,
Love flourished and then surpassed
Any of my limited verbal concoctions.

For even with electronic clouds of information
That proliferates without any abate
The world's servers will never fully create,
      to communicate,
How finding your love in '58,
Sealed our gates, assisted by heaven's fate.

I've found no means (except with poems)
      to contain or explain
how you've expanded my heart's treasure.
There will never be a tally to score our love,
Using any man-made source or measure.

Love continues,
Roland 04/02/14

(04-02-14)
My verses found are to replace
A greeting card with a Hallmark's face.

ENTER OUR DOOR, #54

We've ventured together to reach and open
Small gifts, plus verses, as a token
Of special words that need to be spoken.
    HEAR THIS:
My declaration of love to you remains unbroken
With each morning we find a gift as we awaken.
Knowing our love continues is
Contained within our waking hearts' strong sinews.

How can your wordsmith be capable to now generate
Those finest words that will then relate
And then convey for both of us to contemplate,
Deepening emotions that continue to resonate.

Ever since we met in late fifty-eight,
We could have never forecast or anticipate
Discovery of the gift of love so fortunate
Now we've known blessings infinite.
Your invasion of my heart did permeate
And was a fulfillment gift, my treasured soulmate.

Within our lives' commotion
Our chosen devotion became frozen.
Your reciprocal love emerged,
And with its returning
Became a profound and tender yearning.

We're continuing our lives' journey with its progress
Within a shared faith we profess.
Thus we are able to go forward
Toward a horizon,
Traveling along the paths we've chosen.

Each day as we continue our devotion
Our love is secured with mutual emotion
The gifts of love that we exchange
Will steadily be a nurture
For our life's adventures
That will complete our futures.

Love, R.

LOVE IS GOLDEN by RGP
(April 2014)

You are my only one since '58 when we found
Fun in the sun and a date with fate.
We found a gate (and did not hesitate) to create
Our love, huge as <u>TEXAS</u>, embracing both of <u>US</u>.

To count grains of sand or ocean beaches only teaches
How vast is love's treasure
That we can never fully measure.
It's only found in countless ways
When our love did embrace and then extend,
Binding us forever and caused to transcend
Life's array of events,
Found on paths that twist and were bent.

We truly savor the flavor of total devotion,
Never detoured by distortion of commotion.
Ever constant with faithful emotions,
More rewarding than man-made potions.

There are precepts proclaimed thru the ages,
Described on paper by wandering sages.
Some proclaim love is a passage of life's seasons
Varying, and not fully bound by solid reasons.

However, these wandering minstrels never
        Found the gifts of true love,
The most treasured gift of all
That will surpass any verses etched on a wall.

Let it be told that truest love,
               Like refined gold,
Will never depart from our hearts
So—constantly and true, I'm in love with you!
I'm yours to have and to hold,
Secured and bound by our love,
Ever to cherish and never perish
Enlarging our joys yet to unfold.

P.S. Wouldn't you know it—
You're stuck with a poet
And the way he wrote it.

Love always,
Roland

THE "ONE"

Only you can be "the ONE"
When all has been said and done.
For you are, for me, like moon and sun.
You are steady and sure in your
        giving and creating
Our family's foundation permeating.

Your constant love, always willing
Nurtured and sustained us, thus fulfilling
The first tributes I'll be bringing;
Because you've kept my heart strings singing.

My heart cannot be displayed to show it, and—
Never finding enough words to compose—
        as your poet.
Your presence is the essence of perfume so rare
Invisible, but always there,
Uniting and sustaining the love we share.

Love Roland
04-22-14
(When returned from sister trip)

DEVOTION
(Mother's Day 05-11-2014)

When the calendar announces "MOTHERS DAY"
The challenge means, "What can I say?"
     (as a verbal bouquet.)
Fathers, sons and daughters all seek to relay
Meaningful phrases and thus display
Their hearts' collection of affection on this day.

The poets ever declare there's no love so true;
And songs are written to thank and renew
The tributes to that tender maternal hold,
That binds a family's hearts as years unfold.

Flowers may arrive, plus loving words on cards
To celebrate the mother who guards
Her family's pathways, from each infant's rocking;
While TIME marches on toward a future unlocking.
She will be directing and protecting with an
     Ever steady love imparting
Preparations for the roads of life; on them departing.

Her husband observes, ever-admiring
The loving skills of a mother's devotion untiring,
While words are blending to my poem ending
I find there remains words I would be sending,
About my love that never falters—
Always certain time _never_ alters
My hearts' gratitude; for your love ended my solitude.

REMEMBERING CHRISTMAS

We say it is time for Santa to gather round
His reindeer with tiny hooves to pound.
From rooftops to ocean isles
Bringing gifts and joyous smiles,
Spreading yuletide cheer, far and near.

But in the moments come other sentiments.
The Wise Men's gifts for the Christ Child meant
Began our gifting from their spiritual uplifting.
We're to recall again "THE REASON FOR THE SEASON."

With the Christmas season drawing near,
The events of our Christmas joy we'll employ.
Using songs repeated in our annual joy.
Forever recalling the images we hold
With special stories again re-told—
These special moments treasured like gold.

RGP
2014

Your constant Christmas spirit, ever-giving and sharing
Leads me to be ever-caring <u>about</u> you and <u>for</u> you.
My failing is that "Thank yous" are too few.

There are timeless ventures love will always need,
And some best intentions do not succeed.
Now's the time to record and proclaim
That my heart carries <u>only your</u> name.

From Ft. Sam and across oceans vast
Your name became deeply cast
Poured into my heart like molded gold, there to last;
As a daily treasure, beyond measure as years go past.

As we travel onward thru our daily maze,
We cherish rewards that come when the heart obeys.

A MOTHER'S DAY TRIBUTE
(2015)

There is a special niche reserved for a mother
That can never quite be given to another.
A mother's life-creation is a certain treasure
That surpasses our abilities to measure.

It is not just the "MOTHER DEAR" that we revere.
FOR—as a wife becomes a mother,
Her husband perceives inheritance from
      THOSE MOTHER'S PRIOR;
ALWAYS directing life's skills to acquire,
Continuing the love, devotion and guidance,
      never available for hire.

The husband fortunate to observe their children mature
Realizes that maternal nature steady and sure,
Enlivened their achievement, far beyond
      What they once were.

A poet once famously wrote, "No poem will
      ever be as lovely as a tree."*
My next phrase you will find to say:
"There will seldom be any other soul
So well-remembered on each Mothers Day"—
As my wife, Bonnie.

With love always,
Roland (2015)

*Joyce Kilmer

THE EPIPHYTE LAMENT by RGP
04/20/15

Rain rewards the swinging Spanish Moss
Never ever assigning the slightest gloss.
But we're not able to function like an epiphyte
We need <u>more</u> to survive and grow in height.

How will we continue to live and thrive?
We'll add in protein and tasty carbohydrates,
Carefully so none of it over-saturates.
Food philosophers we will tolerate
As they initiate their food debate.
But their diet of words will never satisfy or abate
With pet theories and opinions heard early and late

"TRY MY GRAPEFRUIT DIET!" (I can't wait),
Making an addition to list of foods I <u>hate</u>.
Be sure to add pepper, paprika and garlic
(As you fix fancy menus to your slate) - BUT
Continuing with nutmeg, poppy seeds and cinnamon.

All these and more can be found in Mother Nature
Ingredients added we learn to alone abhor.
But will ask you on bended knees
Please cancel those choices causing me to wheeze or sneeze

And now we'll conclude without being rude
That we have accepted flavors we choose to use
Perhaps adding coffee, tea or booze.
Now we declare: 'GLAD WE'RE NOT EPIPHYTES"

To compound our diets we'll prepare
More than simple moisture and air,
Never gimmicky from the pantry's lair
Let's fill our plates with simple fare:
POTATOES, STEAK and PIE.
Then we'll depart with a sigh, "Bye Bye."

Our dietitians will boldly scold,
Our choices are with multiple calories hold
So to conform, with egg whites we'll fold
Into a waiting sugar-free jello mold.

Now becoming wise and older
We'll spoon out oats that have been rolled over
Thus ends my food epistle, AMEN.

WORDS INCURRED
(04-30-15 #1)

I'm prepared to send you a written word,
          perhaps absurd
Knowing the possible pain insured.
Hoping to cause you to gain after the
          pain you've been in.
So perhaps these words are hardly worth a dime
Using my handy thesaurus
I'm prepared to write you a chorus
Combining silly words never to bore us.

As I untie the knots on my bag of thoughts
I've discovered words to create verse absurd,
With a few chosen words to create
What will it take to create verse perverse?

Only a poet would ask you to consider
If you would savor with a cola on your granola
As if to say since it is a rime, it would be
          a tasty time.

It's nonsense you say, but hear me out
For as our advisors often say
A bit of humor should fit into each day.

RGP

RIME TIME
(04-30-15 #2)

You can have my rime every time
For only the payment of a thin dime.
Nothing is free from my verbal menagerie.
Paging through my trusty thesaurus
There are plenty of verses for my chorus.
If the words can be set to the meter,
They will escape the poet's deleter.

It's nonsense you say, as you pay
But hear me out—for they say
A bit of humor is needed for each day.

Using his pen as a clever lever as applied
Again emerges, no longer able to hide,
Thus the word juggler is satisfied;
A bit of humor never ever denied—

No doubt he's un-tieing the knots on this sack of thoughts;
He's lured another word for his verse absurd
He's off and writing with a new matrix
Stitching his verbal quilt with a mix
            of words to fix
Dispelling any frown now unwound.

RGP

WORD-BENDERS UNITE!
(4-30-15)

Behold your wordsmith rhyming words having no aim
Beware! You may be caught playing this game!
Our English glossary has words galore.
There's a vast array in our verbal store.
The challenge is to never be a bore
Bending words to uses never heard before.

Can we now hail the postal person a MAIL LADY
People may feel we've created confusion.
For now the greeting must be a MAIL PERSON.
Thus we find the PERSON BOX filled with mail
Or do we imagine a knight in shining armor male

There is no end to a word-bender's favors,
It's a game using word flavors with no waivers
Creating verbal grits, hash or succotash
From our thesaurus of words that gnash.
All are fair game to mix or patch
Creating a crossword of verse without a match

The rewards are few and often fleeting
When a mis-match becomes a greeting
Other word-benders may stop and bicker
But only since they wished to have been quicker

The risk for these word actions is inherent
Though not really apparent.
But now a word juggler is arrested
        By a verbal purist,

Then appearing before a literary jurist,
Is then sentenced to be impounded
      In a language laboratory.
Now—deprived of pen and pencil in this purgatory
They'll be plagued by constant hallucinations,
Dreaming of their emancipations
When finally given a proliferation of paper and pens

FINALLY! They can resume their writing caper,
Limited only by their supply of paper.

RIMIN' SIMON
(04-30-15)

Let's go find RIMIN' SIMON and turn him loose,
So he can bombard our ears with verbal abuse.
What do we have to lose?
There's no limit to words he'll choose
Crafting verses that make us muse.

He'll never present words that lite a fuse
OR drive us to gather in church pews.
He's just paying his dues
Throwing words together, two-by-twos.
The careful language we often use
Will now be combined into verbal abuse.

He'll easily match and dispatch a batch
With words that he can mis-match,
No fear of history being aghast
Then sent to repent.
He pleads guilty to verbal latching
Using extraneous words he's hatching.

There's no recompense or good defense
For English teachers who take offense
To complain that doggerel will displace good language sense.
They will insist for now and even hence,
We must be proper in every verse we commence.

NEAT WORDS WE MEET
(4-30-15)

Empty your lockers, find your DOCKERS ®
Leave with no seams askance
Because we're headed to a dance!

You pay a toll to rock and roll
But if your pants become rent
You'll be to the bleachers sent.
We'll want no incident of indecent intent.
Let's also not hurt our shirt
And with upper body bare
And be escorted from this affair.

Let's not cheat or delete with words not neat.
Our mis-matches will be unending
Because further creations are pending.
We'll not try to be wise or despise
Literature we studied with elbows bending.
We'll try never to be offending
So there'll be no one who'll be sending
Erstwhile authors far away for some superintending.

LET IT RAIN
(4-30-15)

Let us not watch the rain with disdain
Dodging the raindrop causes us no pain,
For we see the flowers pretty petals gain.
We also see head-high sugar cane
Growing along our Valley lane.
If the rain is not seen on our window pane,
We'll not see our crops remain
Growing well, thus our lives to sustain.

What else will be found in disrepair?
When did our cupboards become so bare?
We'll now be short on veggies for preparing
OR lettuce leaves for salad tearing.
Nor will we see our neighborly hare
Running through our yards, here and there.
And no cotton bales will be there to snare
Then woven into clothes we can wear.

So—be happy when you see the rain fall
On our homes, yards and shopping mall.
Let's hike to the gym and then play ball;
So we'll not be found totally dismal.
Also we could gather at the music hall.

Let the grass grow tall along the wall
And give the mower man a call.
We'll just start another verbal rhyme
To keep us shy of mischief time.

IS THE WORD MIGHTIER THAN THE SWORD?
(04-30-15)

Let's not be bored out of our gourd
With verses reviewers have adored
Let's scramble and mix words from a verbal hoard
Re-using words in combos that have been ignored
Let's cut away word-knots and head toward
Verses said to be mightier than the sword.
Should you be laffing at our verbal gaffing
We'll enjoy the fun you're having.
We find entertainment by poking in the
          Verbal establishment,
With no reason to relent
Since we possess no ill intent.
We're merrily on our way and cruising
Creating some new rimes for our choosing.
Now if we are guilty of confusing
The standards of poetic license
Charge us with jumping the fence
For we're about to commence
Uniting more verbal incense
With an odor intense
That causes people's absence.

"Nothing is simple," says the lady with the dimple
Pans won't fit into my RV sink pit.
"So what's to do with pans so few?"
Making tasty favorites takes all my wits!

The poet then says (with tongue in cheek)
Using phrases suitably oblique,
"ALL'S WELL THAT ENDS WELL."
That may be true and things turn out swell—
But, I have to make all my goodies sure to fit
Into the small pans I use before I can quit and sit

Thus any RV kitchen chore has to be done before
More recipes come marching thru the door,
Begging to be ready so all can raid
The delightful morsels that tickle our taste obeyed—

Love,
R.

It matters not if your road is a golden beat
Or simply composed of gravel or concrete.
So you travel on routes toward goals you've set.
Be certain your efforts are wisely spent.

Motivation is said to be an ethical and valid key,
As you attempt to see what your best outcome will be.
Hidden in a forest of choices are life's chess pieces,
When the right moves are found, your spirit releases
And these goals create new roles, building our souls.

The matrix of people we meet are threads in our life.
They may bring great joys or painful strife.
Our lives' brief hours, hastening on,
          measured by a pendulum's tock and tick,
Mentored by people we choose and pick
These threads as woven, emerge as our life's fabric.

As we discovered numerous choices to select,
Our people-thread fabric emerges with the
          numerous lives we intersect.
Thus are created complex patterns, combining all our lives
With hope eternal our loom of life succeeds
Weaving family and friends in words and deeds.

FOR KNOX COLLEGE CLASS OF 1955
60TH REUNION

Roland
April 2015

ODE TO DOROTHY WHARTON
(KNOX CLASS OF 1955 SEC'Y)

So here's to the class secretary
Known by all to be a rarity
Toiling unseen at her given tasks,
There's been no spotlite in which to bask

Prompt and thoughtful, always sending,
Filing the news of classmates unending—
She deserves our finest accolade
Until we can make her better paid.

"TEMPUS FUGIT" Do you need LATIN to get it?
Comes the truth, "TIME BEARS US ALL AWAY."
We're just penciled in, as they say,
Only here—day-to-day

The ad-writers give us tuneful earfuls
With witty ditties one of their effective tools.
Shall we choose their newest appealing fashion?
                (Driven by their advertising passion)
Better for us a classic style,
Where styling still will bring a smile.
And those fashions stay with us awhile;
Not soon sent to the Goodwill aisle.

We're often hearing flashy philosophy
Peddled urgently in a strident Monday.
Politicians give us exhortations with some fog
With outright lies, with a great divide
Revealed with more truthful research to guide.

They would like us to forget the enormous U.S. debt.
As if to say, "The more you spend, the more you save."
Surely math teachers should stand and rave.
The ad people would urge you to spend with no end
So with your easy credit score, then you'll spend.

FORT SAM, OUR ANNIVERSARY

It was a bright day when we met
For August in San Antonio is seldom wet.
Our first stay there was so brief,
But we were woven into a net
Of affection increasing, and leading us to find,
New emotions that would bind us and never unwind.

We now own a treasure, impossible to measure,
And as our paths we recall with pleasure
Became chapters in our lives, they re-assure
Our love exceeded any misfortunes we were to endure.

So as the years now, numbering "eighty-plus,"
Allow us to review and discuss—
Our mutual love we've found captured and controlled us—

RGP July 2015

REFLECTION TIME
08/20/15

TIME washes over us, there's no denying
While fortunes were sought with thoughts and sighing.
Lofty goals and worthwhile trips meant some
                    special good byeing.
There were (sometimes) the sounds of a person crying

SO—Visited by the fleeting seasons of our life,
Goals were pursued and some encountered strife
There were surprises, but also rewards
As events were composed like musical chords.
Memories thus combined were leading us towards
A completion of life's puzzles as our time affords.

Life's complexities as they were comprehended
Caused us to detour (at times) from paths intended.
Even some valued goals become suspended,
Until a more suitable time was recommended.

All too soon we reach a promised leisure
We watch as others now set the pace of time and place
                    as they measure.
Our observations may not now have an
                    ultimate pertinence,
As emerging aspirations arrive using
                    new determinants.
Thus the pursuit of accomplishments continue,
                    but not by accident.

Love, Roland

Our venerable pipe organ is now retired,
Replaced with electronic memory cards we've hired and wired.
There will always be some sounds with this memory
That could command, be mellow or slightly merry.

The craftsmanship of precisely-fitted plates and dowels
Transferred notes from a page into melodic vowels,
Through hidden pipes of wood, lead and tin,
Now—they'll not be heard again.

It's first voice was heard in Kansas, 1895,
Then restored in Fairfield to again emit sounds alive.
Now keys, stops and pipes will become a memory
With recollections only temporary.
The new collection of electronic coding
Will be revealing sounds for our beholding.

Through years of preludes, hymns, marches and funeral tiding,
The craftsmanship to produce these sounds
is now almost consigned to hiding,
Where a few artisans are still constructing
The queens of instrumentation for worship and presiding.
Electronic reproduction will now become our norm—
As songs and tributes emerge in a new form.

Roland G. Peaslee 08/25/15

Here's to Alvin who greets from behind HyVee meats.
He'll give a ready wave and a smile
As you walk by him from the aisle.
Perhaps he'll have two jokes for passing folks.

He'll still have lots of yard to mow,
But we'll certainly want him to know
That he'll be missed from our list
Of favorite people not seen as often,--
Though not forgotten, we might think he's loafin'.

We want to be certain that he'll know
His honey-do-list will increase and grow.
Though he'll not be at HyVee posing,
Now he may choose to be dozing.
Maybe we'll find him near the coffee lurking,
When he's not found somewhere else working.

R. G. Peaslee, 09/07/15

I wonder as I wander
Out under God's sky—
How wondrous a gift is love's tie,
As we feel "our time" flying by.

We desire good times and joys to last,
Caring and sharing as days go past.
When awake in the night
Our minds strive to hold tight
To that which we found so right.

We know we'll find no potion
            (or rubbed-on lotion)
That will banish sadness, or—
            cause it to vanish.
We've learned we're not able to discern
What lies ahead beyond the coming turn.
Thus, at times, we yearn for a bell,
Which sound announces: "ALL IS WELL,"
Our fears thus to dispell.

Though we may wait, then hesitate
            (hoping not to be late)—AND—
Seek a rewarding gate
To reveal paths, new—for us to pursue.

We're prepared to accept life's unfolding measures—
Then mix them with our memory's treasures.

Love on Christmas Day—2015
(chapter one)

Day-by-day our love has grown
Becoming a mutual gift we've shared and known.

We explored side-by-side on shore and in town,
Never knowing the future hid a wedding gown

Our love remains constant like stars in the sky
          while life rushes by.
And—as stars have always served as guides
Our love continues steady and with us resides.

After FIFTY-SEVEN Christmas seasons have occurred,
And we're glad and happy love endured,
Knowing no crystal ball could have been found
Predicting our love would become sealed and firmly bound.

So as we share this Christmas time,
Here's my poetic rime:
My ever deeper affection and love rings true!
My heart speaks of my enduring love for you.

THE GIFT OF LOVE
(chapter two)

Your gift of love presented to me
Is always present and revealed daily.
My secure base amid life's uncertainty.

However many details arrived for you to mold,
Revealed as our book of life did unfold.
Your skills prevailed and always well-controlled
Thus gifts of our love became more refined,
With our goals defined, and then aligned.

There were always myriad choices to be made,
And through them we found a love without fade.
We will never know a hesitation.
We'll always treasure our Christmas love with celebration.

RGP 2015

CHRISTMAS MEMORIES FOR BONNIE
(chapter three)

For you I've composed this short verse
That will take only a small
                    space in your purse.
I'm giving you short rows
            of rime,
Reminding us of our first
                    Christmas time.
Our first wired up limbs
            of cedar
Avoided a fee for a tree.

We could not make our
                    cranberries and popcorn glow,
But we were content and
                    happy to know,
We had no need for
            any mistletoe.
We could deliver a
            kiss and never miss!

With constant love,

Roland

THE "WHY" of HAPPY NEW YEAR

<u>You</u> have always created my HAPPY NEW YEAR
All days seem so much better when you appear.
It is contentment when you are near.
There are never words enough to proclaim
                    that you are dear.

This year is close to the end of our "RV HISTORY."
Our journeys were not to unravel any mystery.
We just possessed a constant wanderlust.
Our RV's stayed on the move
Through trips that had breaks, leaks and some
                    even caused rust.

It's easy to find sights in Canada and USA.
Mountains, plains and oceans are ever on display.
With pleasurable views, plentiful along the way.

So fill the tanks, check the tires and pack the compartments.
With TOM-TOM in hand, we'll be ready for
                    What the road presents.

RGP 12/31/15

P.S. I love you, Bonnie!

Our busy lives have faced both concerns and chores,
We found life presented new challenging doors.
But even as we encountered those
        "WHATEVER FORS"
We found rewarding good times, even including
        SMORES.

Your loving devotion to our family's goals
Assisted their defining of their life's goals.
Our family thrived, expanding skills and souls.
Now passing years will reveal
The continuing tally of achievement totals.

My rimes will attempt, using verses clever,
To continue my heart's promise of love forever.
As we stroll along LOVE'S AVENUE,
My cherished memories of love will always be:
        YOU.

RGP
02/16

Life unfolds for our journey to a further place
And our life together renews my heart's pace.
Just to see your smiling face
Makes it a better place.

You should know how much better my world
                    came to mean
When you enter life's varied scene;
And nothing has ever come in between.

There are passing events that emerge
                    as memorable pleasures,
But nothing comes close to your natural gifts,
                    beyond all measures
creating deepest heart-warming treasures.

Since your arrival awakened my latent passion,
Enhanced by your timeless kindness and devotion.
We now know our love has shown no
                    decrease or moderation.

As we continue our lives <u>together,</u>
With continued binding of life's ideals,
We wish for no repeals.
Our love has surpassed any fleeting fashions;
Thus we continue discovery of love's sensations.

(FOR THE DAY CALLED VALENTINES)

Love, Roland
02/2016

DISCOVERY IN TEXAS

Now we have become each other's best friend
        and loving soul mate,
An outcome we could have never known to anticipate,
And how our TEXAS encounter would begin in
        NINETEEN FIFTY-EIGHT.

With my return following our KOREA KORRESPONDENCE
From our different paths we overcame uncertainties.
Proceeding thru the years, we now enjoy family legacies.

FAITH, HOPE and LOVE are proclaimed to be
The secure and certain anchors to build lives of integrity
We became custodians of the lives created
Hopefully guiding those souls thus initiated.

Rewards in our lives defy precise measurement.
Life's inherent incidents arrive without precedence,
But we were able to combine them in coincidence.
"MAKE LEMONADE FROM LIFE'S LEMONS" (or irritations)
This action overcame challenges and situations.
As events were met, and then surpassed,
Our love was the sweetener in life's hourglass.

As we journeyed along life's mileposts,
We enjoyed trips thru prairies, mountains and seacoasts,
Leaving memories vivid, often miles of signposts.

But now, as we shrink our future tally of RV miles,
We have countless recollections and smiles
When we recall seeing grizzlies, bison and crocodiles.

Our motorhomes allowed us chosen routes to uncover
Panoramas of mountains, plains and cities for
                   us to discover.

Now, countless scenes in our memories remain to hover;
Allowing us to reminisce and recall
How our meeting in San Antonio began it all.

Our two lives blended in a mutual converging
Leads us on as we continue our constant
                   love and devotion—
With no diverging.

Love, Roland
February 2016

OUR TIME
OH YOU BIRTHDAY! STAY AWAY!

But this request the calendar cannot obey,
For come what may, our day will play,
And perhaps even more memories will stay.

<u>My</u> birthdays have been better ever since
You touched my heart with love's unique pinch
Soon—"OUR YEARS" will total FIFTY NINE
As we continue with lives entwined.

Our realms of dreams we pondered
Became re-combined as we wandered.
Our journey has found joys in
                our faith and love evermore.
Our reward for opening love's special door.

For March 25th 2016
Love always,
Roland

[on card: Truly Yours in Love, Roland (Husbunny)]

YOUR GIFT

Poems seldom arise from fears to tears,
But emerge from emotions that endears.
In our lives, certain gifts do appear
              and never disappear
My rhythm and rimes become combined,
              and further re-aligned—
(With some phrases left behind).
Final words unwind, defined and refined;
<u>Then</u> written verses can be signed.

On this special date the author will not hesitate
To announce this tribute to his soul mate:

It is my goal to leave behind
Verses that relate to the role
Tenderly played by Bonnie, who touched my soul.

This author will ever be bold and never withhold
Constant thanks for this person, so near and dear
Whose tender love was her gifted role
That made me a person whole.

April 2nd, 56th anniversary,
2016

Loved by me, RGP

146

FOR ALL MOTHERS

The day called MOTHERS, among all others
Provides reasons for honor in all seasons.
The gift of a mother's love extends from "ABOVE,"
In a class that no other can surpass.

From the first day, with a babe in arms,
A mother cradles, feeds, soothes and charms
Washing tiny feet and hands cause happy sounds
Among the rewards of happiness beyond all bounds

As years are spent giving love with no relent,
Mother's guide young hearts with loving sentiment.
Then with a grateful soul, searching for a deeper sense,
Comes the question—
How to show thanks for the love so intense?

Flowers, candy, gifts and calls from far distances,
Are tokens of love recalled from so many instances.
The deeply-felt emotions defy all measures
Reserved forever in our hearts' treasures.

Love, Roland
For May 8, 2016

Suddenly into my life you came,
And my days and nites were never the same.
Your arrival with a name that defines "APPEAL,"
Took over my vacant heart; yours to steal.

No lady had become real to me after 1955,
When my affection trip ended after a six year dive

Your wonderful role caused FATHER'S DAY
            ONE, TWO, THREE, FOUR.
Your love always formed the core
That evolved to exceed any tale of love known before.

Know that our lives together have never been oblique—
Never meek or empty as we went on to seek
Another year's rewards, week after week.

How do we now count the blessings we've found?
We'll not choose scores of musical sounds,
            money in mounds or weight in pounds
We're found the gifts of love exceeded the normal bounds.
Thus our lives were used, created and we wove
Patterns formed using FAITH, HOPE and LOVE.

From Roland 06/19/16

YOU ARE "THE ONE"

I love you just the way you are—
                    Near or far.
Day-by-day, you <u>are</u> "THE ONE."
From the first day we met,
Leading on to events and fun.

NOW—as the years roll on,
With all the happenings we have done,
There is a recall, with pleasure, the treasure,
That it was my heart you won.

SO, "YES"—you will always be, "THE ONE."

Love, Roland 06/19/16

Even today the San Antonio River still flows,
Attracting visitors who seek to make a pose.
In another time, it was not a place anyone went
For at nite there was a risk of a body being "bent."

While north at Fort Sam, a world away,
Interns and doctors were busy every day,
Fulfilling contracts with requirements to obey;
Preparing to go wherever U.S. orders would say.

Arriving from Iowa and Illinois came a girl and a guy
Their commissioning contracts to satisfy.
There were courses of study to be advised,
Before their next assigned duties would be realized.

There were a few dates and Earl Abel's for cake or pie,
Plus a trip to the Gulf for this girl and guy.
They found Mustang Island, accessible by ferry
And the sleepy town of Port Isabel, there to tarry.

Too soon the guy's orders arrived; Korea duty contrived
Months passed by with letters written,
Writing quick notes between duties smitten.
Special thoughts were penned on fragile pages
And thru various stages there developed
                    mutual "affection gauges."

When together again, arriving at CA's Oakland Bay,
It became for them a special day along life's way.
When they would know their paths combined
                 would never stray.

Now fifty-six years allow them to declare
There has been a fast pace (at times)
                 For this pair.

But even with life's wear and tear,
Were those years the cause for
Heads of white hair?

Love, Husbunny

Call us Winter Texans—that's who we are
We sing in the valley, near and far
When we're on the risers, we're up to par.

You can hum your "whiffen poof" song
And other ballads that have come along
We have songs with clever verse at the ready
To sing for you with verses clear and steady.
Give us a listen
For we m ay cause a tear to glisten.

But as we continue to sing for you
With verses sweet or melancholy
Switching at times to celebrate or be jolly
You may hear us sing "Hello Dolly."
Broadway, spirituals, or a patriotic song
We'll present them with gusto
Even invite you to sing along.

For anywhere we chose to roam
You'll hear our chorus sing our theme
"We love our valley home."

Roland Peaslee, Senior Ambassador Chorus

March 2016

Here in the valley called RIO GRANDÉ,
There are some things we miss from IOWAY.
The snow is certainly NOT in our futures
But we are also less likely to need sutures.
Falling on the ice is just a recollection
As we recall salt trucks making a street selection.

SEEING <u>PEOPLE</u> MAGAZINE totally in Spanish
Tells us how here, we've seen English almost vanish.
Yo-Yo weather has come to the land.
First there's sweat, then find a jacket and hat in hand.

They say last summer was 100° plus with the
                    humidity high,
So when April arrives, we'll leave with a sigh,
Glad to go home, wave to you and say, "Hi!"

RGP, 7 Dec '16

Poems are "showems," brief expressions
             with thoughts revealed
To record praises hastily concealed.
"Time flies," as we learn so well,
And caring for someone we love creates
             treasured memories, to forever dwell.

Creating phrases that rime, like an enzyme—
Enabling, facilitating to thus combine
Pleasant chords like a musical score,
             and then:
From our mind's eye, we lovingly recall and explore
The complexities we found in that
             unique person we love and adore.

With erosion of our creative edge (or skill)
The poems remain—a tribute on each page,
             and thus exists to fill
The gaps in expressions along life's paths,
             somewhat "down hill,"
No longer able to contrive a vivid recall
             but refusing to mope—
We affirm again, how fortunate was the
             Gift of love received, helping us to cope

For Bonnie Dearest,
Christmas, 2016 (by RGP)

THE <u>OTHER</u> CHRISTMAS GIFT

We know Christmas arrives once each year,
But with your persona wonderfully near,
Each of my days found fulfilling cheer.
Your love and companionship was so sincere and dear.

Any return to Texas always brings me
                a vision, that tells me—
You have been the other reason for the season.
Now with these 58 years now passed,
We've known our future began in Texas:
         San Antonio, leading to our Iowa home thus:
Your love has always been a recurring
         theme for any poem.
You endowed our lives with love given
         with <u>every</u> sun rise,
Providing countless skills, weaving
         lasting family ties.

Now—viewing our quilt of memories—
         we continue to recognize and realize,
Family ties of love were secured each day,
With faith that knew no compromize.

Love, always—
Roland, Christmas, 2016

TO MEASURE OUR TREASURE
by RGP for 02/14/17

We face a challenge to create a defined tally or measure
Suitable and unique, to define LOVE'S TREASURE.
Ranging far and wide,
Bound with our special love, side-by-side;
No monument erected will suffice
To document our love-secured splice—
Totally binding our lives, secured by love's surprise.

We entertained no pretense or disguise,
As we were to realize
We could see our future, combining our lives.

NOW—with lives in a holding pattern of lymphoma code
        That defines our current events mode—
We now review those passing years using love's code
Stitching a fabric of events having sewed.
We've created a quilt of memories that
        never disappears—
This is our treasury, measured now with
        many joys and a few tears.

Our treasury of love grows fonder still
As new events occur, and then distill,
Additional patterns for our lives' quilt.
Thus we envision our families' lives
        continuing to fulfill.

Written 01/28/17

Cupid's arrow flew in San Antonio,
And our lives began a new scenario.
Quietly, but surely, your presence for
　　　　me was found (letter by letter),
A tie that could not be unwound.

Finding you in Oakland, then cradling Carol Ann
Revealed a future for me to see a different man.
Never has there been any doubt
About the total lock, binding our love-knot.

As our years add up, leading us on,
We have tokens of what our love has won.
They carry names for us so dearly known—
Maturing from the love genes we have sown.

Now, with their lives, we're not alone—

RGP 02/14/17

As a birthday does arrive, we face a choice.
Some say this event annoys, others greet it
with calm and poise,
Knowing the gift of time is welcome, always.

In earlier years some found new clothes
or a special toy,
Plus a favorite cake all could enjoy.
Now in the present day of 82 years
We'll choose candles, flowers plus hearty cheers.

Now as that special day draws near,
That requested cake (or pie) is to appear with candles 82,
Correctly counted and all brand new!
Flowers received, always appropriate,
Ever if only lasting a week to appreciate.

Those knowing the honored celebrant
Will send greetings if their travels are a "can't."

RGP 03-25-17

FOR MOTHER'S DAY 2017

We know few treasures that enhance our busy days
On our varied journeys thru life's mage.
So let us join and with thoughts combined
Give thoughts of love for mothers who lives defined
The standards of love in our lives they refined.

Mothers are wives whose patience may be strained
When husbands are short on praise for tasks so well-maintained.

Here's my sincerest tribute to one I know so well:

You've made our lives together so memorable!

Love always,
Roland

For John Klover

As friends are transferred into memories,
Let us compose thoughts that will ease
Our recalls forming a treasury.
Within those virtual pages of life's details
Are varied years of occasions and events—
Ranging from laughter to moments tense.

It will remain a privilege, secure in my mind,
To recall our meeting in 1958, that came to bind
Or lives into new service and duties defined.

As our paths separated over years and miles,
Distance and time never erased those
       memories that generated smiles.

Roland and Jon, friends for 59 years.

Roland

WE TEXAS TWO

There was no plan that could anticipate
Our August meeting in nineteen fifty-eight.
Both of us were hastening along in Texas sun.
Yet FATE found us there and hearts were won.

With gulf shore fun and a new rock lobster taste,
Cupid's arrows were flying with certain haste
For there was no time to waste.
Too soon Army orders arrived unwound
And by November, I was Korea bound.

Letters flew across the ocean blue
With no thought of what Cupid would do.
Hearts grow fond with true affection found,
As words were sent back and forth with no sound.

Now fifty-nine years have flown swiftly by.
We've locked our love into lasting ties.
Preserving treasured memories of our family
We so proudly prize.

Love, Roland
Aug, 2017

As October ushers in an Iowa winter teasin'
We pause to recall our Texas season.
It was the discovery of the love of my life.
She is a treasure, who became my wife.

As time went on past Labor Day, nineteen fifty-eight,
We saw each other often, leading to Nov. eighth.
An officer's club date began a lover's wait.

A year and a few days more found us
      reunited at Oakland's Gate,
About to become more than we could anticipate.
Flying to L.A., thru an eventful New Mexico night,
Arriving at Dallas Naval Air Station—before—morning light.
From there to Ft. Hood, at attention we stood—
Following orders to there do some good.

Fifty-nine years have truly flown past,
And we have found love's blessing will last.
The legacy we see in pictures on the wall
Ever remind us of how it began at a breakfast call,
The beginning of "us" in a San Antonio fall.

Love, Roland
October 24, 2017

TEMPUS FUGIT—DO YOU FEEL IT?

Some say time marches on or flies away, but never stands still.
Are we ready to brace our hearts with a steady will?
The day you designate as only ordinary
May contain events that make the day downright scary.
Will your response be prompt or will you tarry?

Our lives need direction with fulfillment judged by our motivation.
What drives your goals worthy of completion?
As we ignore some tasks we so easily postpone
Know that they may strengthen you for
                    challenges as yet unknown.

"FACE THE FACTS!" Now this is heard, we choose what to do.
Will we choose any shortcuts to reach goals we pursue?
Should we be compelled to retain worthy goals
That secure our souls?

As we create a record of worthy actions,
Strife in our life should allow no distractions.

RGP 11/01/17

They say it is more blessed to give than to receive,
    So <u>they</u> say—however,
Do they know the depth of "Bonnie's Way"?
She gives so much on any given day,
From her first morning moments, awake from sleep,
She never speaks in a dismal peep.

Thru the day her actions are done with a smile;
And then if tired, she rests awhile,
Readying herself for the next action file.
In response to any pressure,
She will always give her full measure.

Precious gems are rated with standards of quality
Bonnie is the true five star reality.
Loved and treasured, highly prized
My love will never be disguized.
Presenting my love for her knows no limit.
My wish is to be better for her every minute.

Bonnie, you became my most treasured gift in my life
When you said you would be my wife.

Love, Roland
Christmas 2017

We're ready to greet the new year with our love intact
This means the world to me, I state that fact.
We've given our love, undivided and true;
And my world has always been better—because of YOU.

Your presence has always been my constant reward.
Your love, the steady force moving me onward.
Day-by-day you've given me your gentle touch,
Your precious gift, never decreasing, means so much.

We've entered another year together
With that bond that will never sever.
I give you my constant love, every time.
So: DON'T FORGET! I LOVE YOU!

Love, Roland
Jan 01, 2018

With Bonnie's Christmas snow wish fulfilled,
Shall we search for more events to remain thrilled.
There are many things, possibly unique arrivals—
But—we are thankful for today's plenty—
      found in the pantry vessels.
A warm home secured with true love pure
Is a wish fulfilled, sure to endure.

As we realize so little of the coming year,
Faith sustains us as we now proceed,
Even if what we find causes the need
To shed a tear for someone we hold dear.

Sustained with our love and faith,
We're called to nurture wisdom that will insure
We'll not be led astray by fantasy,
      or a clever allure.

When the roll is read, and we're called by name,
May we be found secured by faith,
      instead of fame.
We know life is a gift, and not an
      invitational contest game.

RGP 01-01-18

A THANKFUL SOUL
21 Jan, 2018

Oh yes, we're glad for our home, pleasant and warm;
And good friends who will never cause harm.
Also with pantry well-stocked at the ready
With utilities paid—dependable and steady.
Now winter brought us snow and ice,
Yet we're certain spring will return with temps so nice.

We're glad for family who come and call when able,
We're glad as we learn they are enabled and stable.
Though life delivers, at times, a rough patch;
Moving on to meet, defeat and then surpass.

There's my ever-thankful spirit for a devoted spouse,
Without Bonnie, our home would only be a house.
She is the very definition of mother and wife,
Supportive and never a source of rancor or strife.
Rising above life's routines so ordinary
From next to last, always with sound counsel,
       tenderness and love I find exemplary.

Bonnie the gift of hope and love so necessary
Guiding children's best goals to emerge primary.
From cradle to diplomas, she had no vacations
Sewing on medals for memorable occasions.
With wise gentleness, she persuaded passions
       that had invaded.
Her love prevailed with better ideas unveiled,
Encouraging motivations to be successful reactions.

The gift of faith is our asset cast, a gift that will last.
An anchor in our lives, as for those ancestors past.
Whether we work with heart, hands or minds,
It is a steadfast faith that security binds;
Never abandoned as we find our future unwinds.

Our world presents doubts and shifting standards.
So we must maintain worthy safeguards.
If temptations appear with questionable benefit,
We must measure any demerit we could inherit.
Doubts may occur, so we must defend and limit
Actions that could damage or diminish it.
Our faith must remain definite and infinite.

R.G.P.

HELLO BONNIE!
Jan 2018!

No medals for homemaking have been devised,
Though bracelets, necklaces and rings are often advised
But these do not proclaim the regard for daily fares.
Whether swept away or kept for later,
They'll be completed with diligent care.

Making lemonade from life's demands delivered
Is said to make the remedy for plans "slivered."
But with sweetness of love used in home adventures,
Frowns and tensions are eliminated from careless mixtures.

Now we'll plant a forest of trees,
One for each of her gifts labeled "BONNIE'S."
She is my Iowa girl found in Texas,
When a breakfast date turned my life to a new axis.

There were no shooting stars, trumpets or thunder's sound
To announce the special lady that I had found.
But as time and events would reveal
Her heart signal was the unlocking key to our history,
Enabling a future that has been a wonder
        to you and me—

Love,
Roland

AH HA!

What lucky fella has found nearby Bella?
Would Jarrod be his name of track & swimming fame?
Do we hear St. Valentine at the door?
He better not bring a box of rocks!
Candy would be dandy, in a box with no locks
So all would share while the clock tics & tocs.

We knew our love grew soon after we met.
A blending of love and desire followed our event,
With letters over the Pacific sent.
Once begun it was a love affair we could not forget.
So—every kiss since has confirmed our love
       without regret.

We have never lived in a haze or confusing phase.
Ours is a treasured love that binds us thru nites and days.
We have never used pretense or a fake smile.
Our love has shaped our dreams and lifestyle.
Our mutual love has never known denial.

My poem found emotions I've never before voiced;
Since words composed and written are carefully choiced.
This my gift for you from my testimony
To our shared love and committed matrimony.

All my love,
Roland

Valentine's Day surely arrives each year
When flowers, candy and poems always appear,
A reminder of our years past we hold so dear;
Celebrating our love always brings us cheer.

As we wait out Iowa's wintry blast,
We count the days til freezing temps have passed—
For we snows cannot last.
Then spring chores will arrive with demanding tasks.

Our love has known no seasonal variations.
It remains steady and faithful with no vacations.
There will never be enuf phrases placed on pages
To list all the countless ways your gifts of love
　　　　exceeds all gauges.

We've filled our library of love since our pairing
With memorable scenes we'll always be sharing
With a quilt of love we've been wearing.
We own our life's memories in our treasury of affection
There are no erasures or need for correction.
At no time since we've been married
Has our love been side-tracked or buried.
You remain in my heart even when we're apart.
The touch of your lips secures my heart with tender grips.

Whether rain, snow or on a sunny day,
You've made our world better, no matter what came our way.

Soon routes chosen to OROBOJI will have begun
To greet smiling faces at the REHDER REUNION.
Memories and traditions will be in review
Continuing our family's heritage for faces new.

Coming from coast-to-coast, we can boast
This gathering is worthy of a toast.
What began with VERN and FERN
Was like the action of a butter churn,
Shaping several lives into families firm.

Grandpa's belief in a faith steadfast
Merged with Fern's love as the years passed.
With the seventh procession of names now gathered,
We'll show that family surely has mattered.

Games and reminiscing will be a recurrent treat
As we renew bonds of loyalty with no defeat.
This seventh reunion will become complete,
        our traditional repeat.
We'll recall these treasured memories that
        will remain ever sweet.

RGP 02/19/18

When the cancer invades the ductile
Then there's no action subtle for cells so mobile.
Now do the labs and other tests complete
So all those cells will know defeat!

There's no sure science in the world we know
That can prevent naughty cells that grow.
But once they're found we'll end their reign
Allowing all involved to know no pain.

Our best wishes are sent to your door!
Please know that we treasure you more and more!

Love,
DAD 02/23/18

Best I can do on the spur of the moment.

HOORAY FOR JAY!
(For 03/08/18)

Another year is surely beckoning!
It's time for your annual day of reckoning.
By Chinese standards, you were <u>one</u> when born.
But—even if we were to declare you 52,
There would be no reason to be forlorn.
We'll gladly celebrate the special day you were born.

Grade school for you passed by in a snap.
Junior high came and went, filling the gap,
Ready for high school's demands, plus times of fun;
With Boy Scouts, church and cross country runs.

High school's conclusion was a "one-up" to Queen Mary.
With Dr. Tree's speech help, applause came from many.
Off to Gustavus Adolphus, with a degree in finance,
Then off to Denver without a second glance.

There, joining Augustana's choir you were led
To meet Kirsten, with hair slightly red.
Your family grew and left for educations,
Fulfilling requirements for their aspirations.

We're proud to be called your elderly parents
Of a son who has acquired new skills and patience.
Plaudits are given with our sincere praise
To a son who has matured in so many ways,
Keeping useful goals in sight thru life's maze.

Love, DAD

TO OUR 56'ER (ALAN)

You came first, entering our Fairfield scene,
And chose a date that merged between
Prior family birthdays noted in our March routine.

As we noted your hyperactivity, channeling that drive
Led you into activities found, enabling you to thrive.
Scouts, college, ROTC, work and frat leadership
Blended skills toward future admission payment "CHIPS."
You finished your Masters degree,
Then an optometry "DOCTORSHIP."

Your family and your kin are for you worthy causes
Your concerns find no rest or pauses.
Current events have altered the family life's maze
With actions taken reveal your skills in special ways.

Achievements we've known have given us true pride,
Observing your knowledge integration
            and then further combining
A continuation of expanding your professional defining.

With the gift of faith your skills are applied.
With decisions reinforced you thus provide
Sincere concern for family
And those who receive your care, far and wide.

Love, DAD 03/15/18

WE GOT A ROBOT!

Our home robot will now regularly maintain
Routine tasks to retain our household domain.
I-Robot checks each day, finding some tasks the same.
But there are others that remain.

I-Robot turns on the coffee to start our day anew,
Releasing the aroma of our favorite brew
I-Robot sees the birds coming to feed
And fills the feeders with the seeds they need

There are dishes to wash and trash to squash.
Filling the distiller yields water for the air wash.
There are groceries to fetch plus mail to catch.
Bills arrive in a batch, so checks written are soon dispatched.
When sleep arrives,
I-Robot checks to see doors are latched.

Coffee club is a nine fifteen routine,
But we seniors never make a scene
Even when the joke is ribald or slightly obscene.
The daily number game has laffs in between.

Trips for groceries find the robot is soon back,
Placing items neatly on shelves and rack.
On Sundays, Robot joins the choir
Though only nine arrive to the task aspire.

Garbage and re-cycle day comes each week,
And waste management arrives, a load to seek
Such a busy life for Robot and his wife
Completing chores without horns, drum or fife.

As spring soon arrives, we'll hear the songs
      the birds will be making
And garden seeds will soon be awakening.
Mowers and trimmers will emerge to start their tours
With I-Robot guiding them over the grassy contours
This will take precedence over fishing lures.

I-Robot will exchange snow tires for their summer vacation
From usefulness during winter's duration.
Plans for summer travel will begin to unravel
With plans for destinations originating
Using chosen routes and reservations designating

———————

When this erstwhile poet finds words congruent
The results emerge as verse perhaps
      perverse, but hopefully fluent.
With a dictionary of words to choose
A poet can construct with slight verbal abuse
Using words that bind—yet he's not confined
      to utilize only those words sublime.
Unwinding the poetic mind re-defines the re-created rhyme.

———————

If one should travel on US 34 by way of Fairfield,
You'd find words with poetic uses
      slightly concealed or re-congealed
Poets never know what may grow
From an aging mind turning mellow—

R G Peaslee 03/11/18

Our love began the summer of NINETEEN FIFTY-EIGHT
At FT. SAM HOUSTON, there we would matriculate.
One in dietetics and one to learn army regs to stipulate.
One directed food going on patients' plates;
To other learning how army medical records are mandates.

From FT. Sam to Korea, then both had orders for FT. HOOD.
We performed our duties there, doing some good.
Planning our wedding a thousand miles away
Making a trip to SAC CITY for our wedding day.

Our April second was recorded, then off to HOT SPRINGS
Please no puns about honeymoon happenings.
Back in TEXAS, we completed our army contracts.
When discharged, we went to Fairfield to perform eye exams
             and fitting contacts.
We watched Parsons College growth with a pace frantic.

Our first house was 200 HIGHLAND AVENUE.
Alan, the first child to be born in Nineteen Sixty-Two.
Brian in 1964, arrived, plus house remodeling and new office too.
That summer was a blur with so much to pursue.

We finished the west room addition, a completed project
So we would be ready for Jay's birth target.
He fit between other march dates already history
Finding his own date to start his ancestry.

Christmas nineteen sixty-seven came and went
With Jay's birth announcements all sent.

By December sixty eight, Dian arrived for all to see,
So we placed her under the Christmas tree.
My dad reminded me we now had a car full
Providing a space for each family jewel.

Colleges, degrees and licenses earned to begin practice
Were major events for each professional apprentice.
Now their families are glad to receive congrats
Observing progress exceeding routine stats.

On our 58th date, we're trying to be up-to-date,
Living in the Hawkeye State feeling fortunate.
Sometimes we choose to go, or hesitate
Making trips or deciding to wait,
Matching energy levels on any given date.

Overall we enjoy those anniversaries and birthdates
Since they are reminders of special dates that we congratulate.
Now countless destinations we recall,
          memories never to be encased
About challenges we successfully faced,
We review often those motorhome sorties,
Finding distant places and writing our own stories—

RGP 03/25/18

Fifty-eight years is a cause for cheers!
Our love has surely increased thru these years.
We relate with pride how we two grow to six
With genes we combined to become well-mixed.

We were Iowa-born Northwest and Southeast,
But Texas was the place
Where under Texas sun, we met face-to-face.
Though miles soon separated us, we caught a vision
With lives combined by our love's decision.
Though our love began in a time so short,
Our letters become our way to sort
How we two could become one with a joint effort.

Coffee now brewed for me, and tea for thee,
With only slight differences we see.
We find it easy for us to agree.
So we continue our love, you and me.

We can look back on places we've seen
From coast-to-coast Canada, Alaska and in between.
Our FOUR grow up adding "GRANDS" now thirteen,
Preparing for challenges not yet seen—

Surveying the many miles over which we strayed
We re-count those memories that never fade—

RGP 04-02-18

HAPPY BIRTHDAY ALLISON NICOLE!

It's all true and we'll not hesitate
To ring bells and start to celebrate,
We'll cheer for Allison ready to be 25!
With new challenges certain to arrive.

When in Shakespeare's "12th Night" revealed
You, the charming lady so well-concealed
Flashing eyes and long tresses were revealed
The sham was now finally overcome
No more need to conceal or be mum.

And now we know there's a wedding day
To be held in Chattanooga, up Tennessee way,
There to wed Jordan who will not be pale
Ready to start on their marriage trail
As Mr. & Mrs. Jordan Hale.

Now entering new paths, before unknown
Building their future and new skills to hone.
Now lives are better, no longer alone,
Caring for each other will set a new tone
Assisting them both as they form a new home.

RGP
4/12/2018

Now we find KENT by the Air Force sent
To serve and guard, not living in a tent.
Seeking farther ways to cause Radar waves to be bent,
Thus to prevent an unexpected incident.

Fish find out he casts a mean hook
With skills not gleaned from any book.
Now we await this guy
Offering an invite to his fish fry.

Maybe he'll find a sea trout out and about.
When his guests arrive for his fish fry.
They'll be reluctant to bid this fine guy "GOOD BYE."

We think of Kent often in the Florida sun,
While we wait here for spring to have begun.
Then comes grass to mow and flowers to bloom,
Weaving their colors on Nature's Loom,
Perhaps even brightening our living room.

With acquired engineering skills to matriculate,
There's no reason to hesitate,
And further congratulate
Our grandson we see so fortunate—

Grandpa P.
04-06-18

We find an April snow arrived this day
Coating grass and tree limbs as they sway.
But warmer temps will prevail, as if to say,
"BEGONE, YOU LEFT OVER WINTRY DAY!"
This final snowfall will allow kids to play—
Throwing snowballs wishing snowmen cold be alive for a day.

We watch feathered friends seeking seeds to eat.
Snow will delay their nests to complete.
Spring yard chores will also know delays
While we await the return of pleasant sunny days.

Those pesky squirrels, ever clever,
Are on the prowl as they continually endeavor
To rob our bird feeders of their content,
Which are prepared with planned intent
For finches, chicadees and woodpeckers meant.

We observe leafless trees, limbs outlived with snow
Knowing warmer breezes causes snow to fall below
Encouraging the dormant grass to grow;
And a few daring dandelions emerge as a flower show.

We recognize the master decorators seasonal show
Who also directs our lives as we hurry and go—
Coming for all, great and small, short n tall.
Now we will proclaim,
        "THE LORD OF LIFE REIGNS ETERNAL!"

MOREL MYSTERIES

Those who hike, hover and then discover
Tasty mushrooms called MORELS,
Will never reveal the location to find these tasty morsels.

So, off we go into woodlands (to others unknown),
To search out where secretly these have grown.
Will fill our sacks, looking over our backs,
To be sure no one finds our tracks.
Locations where MORELS are found
Become family secrets by honor bound.

Now find the skillet, allowing butter to sputter,
Before those MORELS can protest being dipped in batter.
This springtime ritual is no virtual endeavor.
REALITY arrives when tasting their special flavor!

RGP, April 2018

JENS the 23rd

Now we hear JENS perform with his euphonium
Listening crowds respond with reserved pandemonium.
His performance may be worth a testimonium!

Into the musical world he now parades
Surely to garner further accolades,
As he presents no musical charades.

The notes found on his musical score
Remain there for him to discover,
With his interpretation creating melodies that hover.

A dessert for our ears will be declared.
As his skills never spared create music to be shared.

RGP 2018

BONNIE'S MOTHER DAY, 2018

Mother's Day has arrived for our special attention,
A cause for our tributes with no hesitation.
We're glad to celebrate and thus demonstrate
How this mother's life served to generate
Wise decisions and her devotion did perpetuate,
Memorable actions with results for us so fortunate.

Combining your love with patience and skills,
Maintaining and motivating, to lovingly fulfill
Generational gifts that became condensed,
Directing the family's goals to achieve worthwhile intents.

Her husband watches with love and wonder
As she applies her thoughtful guidance, with no thunder.
He is especially aware, grateful for loving care,
So constantly aware of the love they share.

This poet's thoughts arrive to bind in my mind,
Making me thankful for our special love combined.
For when my heart became assigned to you
It became a gift to me, a daily display, of our love renewed.

RGP
2018

Your gift of love to me exceeded all my dreams.
To list them now would require countless reams.
My heart's treasures were filled by your daily measures
Of enduring devotion and profound emotion.

Re-tracing actions taken during countless busy days
Remind me now how you were the guiding
                    compass in numerous ways—
Always good choices using a steady gauge.
Your familiar question of "READY FREDDY?"
Would be the start of another event to be met unfazed

With metabolic physiology now altered by invasive lymphoma,
We find our time being measured by an invisible "metronome."
A crystal ball, if sought, would prove inadequate,
Even if such an item could be bought.

We know our life together found blessings that were caught,
Plus those life-lessons we found and taught.
Sixty years have added branches to our family tree.
Hopefully strong, steady and useful they will be—

RGP 2018

THE KITCHEN QUESTION:

Who will declare the most useful kitchen appliance we behold?
Will you cite the fridge with freezer cold
OR the induction cooktop, replacing the stove of old!
What will you say of the microwave with buttons waiting
To command penetrating wares with no hesitating?

None of these rate a sustained look,
For entering the kitchen is our loving cook,
"QUEEN OF THE RECIPE BOOK."
She blends the chosen condiments with ingredients
Combining crucial items from her pantry convenient.

By adding her gift of love, never ambivalent,
Numerous skills result in culinary fulfillment—
Thus creating many a fond memory
With the culmination of results now legendary.

RGP 2018

Gather around you brothers three, as sons you also be,
To remind you fatherhood has costs never "free."
From newborns to wedding bells,
Tears, fears and questions of "HOW?" forever dwells.
So it will always be when offspring ask "WHY?"—OR—
"Is this the correct way?" (You will try to satisfy.)
You face many needs (beyond hunger) as they cry.

Guides exist for our trips into unknown areas bound,
Leading to special areas not otherwise found.
But the persistent goal to make decisions called "WISE"
Often reveal feelings of a reluctant compromise.

"BE FIRM BUT NEVER MEAN" was fatherly advice for me,
Maintaining a steady path, a lifelong rule,
Without resort to abuse or loud ridicule.
Ever hopeful to summon measured guidance with reliance
Maintaining FAITH in receiving forgiveness and renewal.
Learning to avoid those tempting side tracks,
We acquire useful lessons from "Life's School."

With passing time, a role-reversal cannot be deferred
As the title GRANDFATHER will now be heard.
Recollections of children who are now descendents
Emerge from our memory banks
Recalling when WE were their parents.

As time lines of family history create challenges anew,
And, as always, harmful emotions must be subdued.
Respect and kindness blended with moral obedience
Create trustworthy family-friends with lasting resilience.

Parenting success grew from seeds bravely sown
Time-tested bonds were created—
Now recognized and securely known.

So our demonstrations of love should be evidences shown
As fatherhood leads us all into a BROTHERHOOD
In love, now well-known.

Love from your dad,
a.k.a. R.G.P., 2018

SAGA of R/F (Refrigerator/Freezer)

The fact accompanying income above subsistence
Compels addition of numerous appliances added to our existence.
Now, challenged by technology's advances,
The task to replace or repair means
Likely taking a few chances.

Faced with R/F failure in the van past week,
Finding the correct replacement requires a peek
Into the space remaining from the appliance removal.
The replacement box must fit properly
In order to receive the final approval.

Enter "MR. FIXER" with several tools inbound
To remedy this replacement challenge now found.
"NOTHING SIMPLE" we always find as details unwind.
Pipes and wines originally secured
Do not match up with new locations, now absurd.

Not to waiver, "MR. FIXER" renews and will re-locate
Braces, holes and wires thus to vacate
Space necessary for the new unit to operate.

With limited space for legs, shoulders and elbows,
In our mini-motorhome small work spaces poses.
With problems of alignment, MR. FIXER knows
It will be a part of installation woes.
What was not predicted was a shoulder sprain;
            (So that's how it goes.)

Now writing verses while waiting to be recovered
Who knows what new repairs are to be discovered?

Shall we return to a simpler existence?
No, we'll agree, with an admittance
We do enjoy the modern convenience
Provided by inventions so ingenious.

It can be stated that time is on my side
To allow healing so pain will subside.
Then once again to crouch and remedy "the situation"
As man overcomes mechanical frustration.

Give the fixer an elixir!
RG Peaslee, 06/07/18

HAIL TO THE CHOCOLATIER!

Let us gather those who savor the flavor
Of the unique chocolate taste with no disclaimer.
We claim to be correctly labeled "CHOCOHOLICS,"
Knowing chocolate drives our taste buds to frolics.

So we'll shout and proclaim, loud and proud
With praises for the cocoa bean's flavor endowed.
From the ARCTIC to the EQUATOR.
We'll enjoy our chocolate HOT, COLD, NOW or LATER!

Anticipation compels us onward
Regularly refilling reserved spaces so fully restored,
Replenishing chocolate supplies in our hoard—
Ready for uses, just waiting in our cupboard.

There are no reasons to be arbitrary or temporary
Recognizing we have no choice but to rejoice
Please save a place for those who have served
Chocolate creations that are preferred.

We'll accept no excuse, even if facing a noose
As we hasten to again taste chocolate so dear
While people gather from far and near.
As trumpets TOOT, we'll stand resolute
Preferring chocolate, accepting no substitute!

We know chocolate may be found combined
With coffee, peppermint and even orange rind.
Those who presume how best to combine—
on any given day—
Tasty chocolate combined in cakes or a parfait?

We welcome the satisfaction
Derived by its extractions
Then crafted with skill and no miscalculations
Thus cooks deliver chocolate unique creations.

RGP 02/18

VIRUS LAMENT

Let's not discuss the ills caused by some virus,
With aches, pains, fever and "SNEEZES."
We'll search for relief that will free us.

From hidden sources seldom known,
A virus emerges our pains to hone;
Until we wear it out and hope to postpone
Any recurrence of what caused us to ache and moan.
We'll not be in denial about our survival
Only hope there are no relatives so viral.

As an illness lowers the boom,
We respond with a bit of fuss and gloom;
And we are often then to assume
It was not our time to push up a flowery legume

Instead of mouthwash, we're back to tea and coffee,
A welcome change we'll all agree.

Be gone you VIRUS! That's our decree!

RGP 07-18

TWIN GUYS SWIM!

You're all wet I'll bet
Preparing to swim and get
Ribbons and medal added to your set.

We're staying dry and we'll try
To stay cool and thus defy
Those predictors who always sigh
That temps and humidity are too high.

We "olde folks" will wait to see
If you succeed to take the lead.
Then your appetites will surely need
Lots of steak on which to feed.

Word-benders like me can annoy
Making words into a mental toy.
We're waiting here in Iowa Land
Ready to lead the band
With no music that is canned.
Think of us as for you we stand.

Grandpa
June 2018

Careful now! Our years are showing!
We know that our love is still growing.
From that summer meeting in San Antonio,
Time has rushed us onward in a scenario.

With time spent at the Gulf and Earl Abel's desserts,
We heard no alarms or warning alerts
That CUPID was present during those days
With bow and arrows ready to raise!

How will we ever explain destiny so illogical?
Was it because of stars and sand—OR—
        Just geographical?
The earth's plates shifted our paths,
Merging so nuptial!

Love for 60 years
RGP 08/18

Whenever at home, hearing those hymns were sung,
Certain ones will linger on our tongue;
Because they recall events and people we've been among.
We recall those ten churches where we've sung,
Where church bells can now be rung.

As Mission Builders, a small claim to fame,
We found new highways, a travel game.
Our motorhome miles meant sights and smiles,
Lingering forever with countless memories the same.

So as LIFE'S grey clouds arrive and depart,
Created memories remain in my heart.
There will never be a day without the thought
Of precious recollections we caught.

TAMA and WALL LAKE, names on the Iowa map,
Fortunately for us came to overlap.
From Iowa to Texas, then our return to this beautiful land;
Always understanding our desire
To return where our lives began,
       and will expire.

RGP
08-18

How will we recall our "IOWA TIME"?
Will we tell it was like steady rolling streams,
Combining life's currents as we pursued our dreams?
Do we recognize the blessings of our life,
Even when confronting life's passing strife?

Luther said, "THE GREATEST GIFT A MAN RECEIVES
      IS THE LOVE OF HIS WIFE."
This message of love remains after a passage of 500 years!
"I LOVE YOU," still the most rewarding words I hear,
Whether whispered or heard thru misty tears.
Poets say our hearts possess hidden strings,
Signaling us when our one special love appears.

As life endows, propagates, celebrates, then separates,
Our sixty years combined events carrying us so fast;
At times we encountered news to broadcast.
Now—retained memories, cast in our past, will forever last.

Iowa was good for early family's pioneering toil,
Living their lives with love for Iowa soil.
The lives they created would continue ever bold
Opening doors to family futures, continuing to unfold.
Our heritage dictates that we create and inspire—
Ever encouraging each new generational desire
To be the receivers of character, inherited and acquired;
Seeking to continue, to achieve and thus re-inspire.

RGP 08-18

BONNIE = LOVE

Being easy to love is your natural way.
This blessing surpasses all others, day-by-day.
We met with only weeks in Texas, then return to "IOWAY."
Our mutual love is sealed forever and a day.

Giving life, forming our family, gifts supreme,
Showing love, plus nurturing, caused children's eyes to gleam.
Their lives have proved a will to excel
Beginning with a mother's love
They now are building lives with more to tell.
They have not forgotten seeds that were planted, so very early,
Now mature in faith, those assets transformed—
      to live securely.

RGP 08/18

Our Love

Should love be celebrated only in February,
When snowmen in our yards are like statuary?
Love discovered, explored, then treasured
Is not limited by seasonal temps we've measured

Love, like a waterfall, plunges into a pool.
We're unable to create a measuring tool
To reach our over-deepening love,
That has surely grown with yearly renewal.

Our love built with the gift of faith,
            became a treasure;
Wonderful to behold, defying any measure.
We've been true and ever-faithful!
We give praises for love and marriage,
            truly bountiful.

RGP 2018—August
The anniversary month of our acquaintance

Our transient winter decorator came last night,
Trimming terrain and trees, fences and bushes
With cottony snow and marshmallow white.
New contours are outlined with adhering flakes,
No duplicates will be found before the sun bakes.
Iowa we know as THE BEAUTIFUL LAND
Rewarding us with memorable views wherever we
     might stand.
We are especially glad when scenery is shared
With a loved one for whom we deeply cared.

From the Mississippi waters to the Missouri's flow
The land between offers a year-long show.
Of prairie heritage is history we know
Enjoying this panorama wherever we go,
Never finding its equal in any U.S. zone, high or low.

The Sac & Fox, Pottawattamie, and Mesquakie
Were the caretakers of this land,
Following nature's guiding hand.
We must also now be stewards of this land with care
For this great inheritance we love and share.

RGP
11-20-18

With zero brothers and sisters in my
family history and cousins widely separated, I read
those articles about "FATHERHOOD"—
    Among those variations I discovered one
that occupied first place forever.
    The way to successfully raise children
is to "<u>LOVE</u> <u>THEIR</u> <u>MOTHER</u>." That simple directive
was certainly on target. With Bonnie, so easy
to love, our beloved four became history.
    "NOW"
Bonnie's watchful eyes, from her picture on the wall
Survey the day's routine chores.
But I hear no "READY FREDDIE?" to announce
    her ready-to-walk or go to the mall.

Her carefully listed items included cards to send,
Yet always she had time a helping hand to lend.
With daily details skillfully rendered
There was never a day with love suspended.

Now with wonderful memories bright and joyful
They are a tribute to her faithful life so WONDERFUL.

RGP
11-20-18

(My mother reading a poem out loud brought its meaning fully)

MY TIME ALONE

My searching has yet to reveal
Suitable phrases with loving appeal
Composed for Bonnie, my poem sequel.

No matter where we found our stopping place
I was always sure of her smiling face.
Slowly now I've formed a haven from the daily race,
Made special in my mind's eye
Forever to be reserved as my "Bonnie Place."

Pictures, verses and fond memories to maintain
Serve to remind—and thus sustain.
Though my heart at times reaches its capacity
For wonderful memories always to contain.

With each daybreak and then the setting sun
Daily I'm reminded of countless joys
We shared while having family fun—AND—
Completion of tasks working as "ONE."
Events we've enjoyed and tasks we've done,
Some in faraway places, never will be forgotten.

Recalling memories so clear provides solace
For my special zone named "BONNIE'S PLACE"
Where we now find FAITH, HOPE,
        LOVE and GRACE.

R. G. P. 11-12-18

My mind comes awake with ideas sifted
As nightmare's shadows are slowly lifted.
What will the new day bring for my attention?
Will choices made be judged by motivations
Because I could go aimlessly with diverted intentions
My time frame seems a contracture, because I
feel a life fracture.
With day's conclusion and tasks completed
Was there time to help others
Or did my choices and actions cause assistance to
be deleted?

Down thru the ages the sages proclaim the virtue
Of providing a helping hand to nurture
Our network of family and friends
Who may create family legends.

In our life EGO may control our survival
As transformers or reformers.
We travel life's complex highways
Choosing to travel in lanes or on causeways
Hopefully complimentary to others in many ways.

RGP
11-20-18

As snow covers our landscape, waiting to answer and grow,
Familiar responses emerge with age-old patterns we know.
We'll recognize duties and chores the seasons will demand;
And we'll choose responses using skills we command.
    But wait:
Now we hear compelling sounds invading our quiet sphere.
Some will be welcome, friendly voices we hold dear.
Conflicting demands will also appear;
We hear words absurd, some causing fear.

Now our reactions will reveal our chosen direction.
If we heed the need for action with defined distinction
Our decision will carve a path, a route of navigation.
Thus we may encounter irritation, temptation and frustration.
As we continue with courage, revealing endurance,
    Suppressing desparation,
The challenge remaining, an answer for our diary notation;
Relating and stating our final justification:
    OUR MOTIVATION.

RGP
December 2018

Our love became attached by a spark from a friend's match
Displacing darkness present along my path.
As we followed our hearts, no tricks in the matrix.
Mutual rewards were revealed, uncovered and discovered.
With emotions unlocked, any retreat was blocked.

To describe my love thru all time, I'll gladly say:
"I LOVED YOU MORE THAN MY
      PRINTED WORDS CAN TELL."
Being with you lifted my spirits any day—
Even if the skies were grey.
Criss-crossing the states over ridges and bridges too
Created constant fun because of you.

There is no way now to leave "Old Fairfield Town,"
For that would surely bring me down.
Carefully stored memories (never erased or blurred)—
Could never again be unwound, restored or transferred.

RGP 01/06/19

THE GIFT OF LOVE WE KNEW

Now arranging words, blending them into rhyme
Recalling October's dusk, that altered my time.
Watching the sunset of this love we have formed,
The gift of love framing out actions, always love-bound.

Our love increased first through a letter-driven romance,
Loneliness eased over an ocean's distance.
The rhythm of love we found grew to our re-uniting profound.
Through FIFTY-EIGHT years we were firmly bound.
We provided for our family, careful to guide,
Lives enhanced to survive any changing tide.

Now there is a family—"modifying,"
As young voices offer help to me, a guiding
Of decisions (that include some reminding)
About new choices to be used for events unwinding.

As sunset began before final darkness became
A symbol of our bond—Bonnie is the name,
Ever a reminder of our love known as a steady flame
Still warms my heart when I hear her treasured name.

When dusk becomes darkness, recollections stay.
The stars seem to be further away.
These recollections, tenderly remembered, recreates
Many smiles we had during our partnered fates.

RGP 01/06/19

FINAL PHRASES

We never felt we were growing "OLD'
Until we were told,
That we would no longer have each other's hands to hold.
Entering this new tunnel of emotions,
With only months to spend,
Caused restless thoughts that would not end.
Realizing we were now forced to process
Our future with no escape sources.

During these months of steady demise
Countless event memories did arise,
A flood of recalling happenings and surprises
Memories from our LOVE BANK were reviewed,
       and then renewed
Forming our unique treasury of joys never subdued;
As only we who were the cast fully understood.

Now listening with my haunted heart,
Bonnie's voice still on my phone
Yields her greeting, so familiar known,
Causes release of several retained tears.
Her voice recalls her life of smiles
Remaining so dear as I begin my solo years.

Here and now, I can read my written phrases,
But speaking those words causes emotional releases,
A reminder we knew our love secure, no detours.
It is impossible to say, "GOODBYE,"
To my forever love, never to deny.

RGP
01-08-19

Christmas cheer this year arrived with a daily tear.
Lites were placed without ornaments on the tree,
Because they were causing many a memory.

FIFTY-NINE years ago our first tree décor
Was popcorn and cranberries on a cord, nothing more.
Our lives had combined with faithful hearts entwined.
Though our future was unknown, we were no longer alone
From Korea, back to Texas, where we had both gone
Recalling our meeting at FT. SAM in old San Antone.

Returning to Iowa in NINETEEN SIXTY,
We set our family at 200 HIGHLAND where the family grew
        with little ones bounced on a knee;
Nightly listening to "GOODNIGHT MOON" after days so busy.
Settled on our big rocking chair arms in pajama wear.
It was part of daily learning how to love, to care
        and to share.
At 200 Highland we began decorating 2 trees for all
        to survey also at 505 Fairway.
Around Christmas treats and presents seen in array,
Many hidden, with no hints given, secure from eyes
Wanting to sneak a peek during Christmas Week.
For all the years not once was there a venture to look
        in the big RV—
Where surprises awaited their disclosure
With glee and hearts made happy.

We saw lives refined and then
        Those lives have re-combined,
Achieving goals they continue to find—

R.G. Peaslee
12/18/18

Spring is the time for concerts. Groups of singers and instrumentalists who have faithfully practised during the winter months invite music lovers to hear their selections.

But consider the songbirds. Free concerts are given <u>every day</u>. Impromptu as they are, they are perfectly executed, with no discordant notes or inharmonious phrases. All are composed on the spur of the moment—and live from year to year, ever new.

Give thought to our friends the songsters. The liquid melodies which bubble from their throats are not to be compared with man-made music. Should only one exist, and appear in Carnegie Hall, admission would be granted only by payment of a princely sum.

For Mrs. Elliff's 80th Birthday,
Feb. 25, 1954.

You still see beyond present-day strife;
You lend inspiration and hope to this life;
Gently you show a way free from fears
With tolerance and calmness gained thru the
Holding great truths close to your heart,
Knowledge and confidence you graciously impart.
May we recognize a challenge and carry on thru
With a lifetime of service, as exemplified by you.

By Dorothy Peaslee, born May 4th 1908

For Bonnie
With love:

Daughters and
        mothers
Have a special
        tie—
We create; we make—
        do—always try—
And on this day—
        set afar—
for honoring Mothers
You capture the
        love we feel—
We've loved you from
        the start!

(From Dorothy Peaslee on A MOTHER'S DAY)

We had arrived under Texas sun, both empty-hearted,
But Ruth and Jon enabled us to be started.
A guy and a lady who were somewhat love-shy,
In only a few short weeks, Cupids' arrow did fly.

Then all so soon, Roland to Korea flew,
And Bonnie was certain he was gone for sure –
Because his goodbye had no overture for a future.
Finally letters began and the two hearts came to discover
That love would entwine with each sunrise's hover.

Now – while snow covers our Iowa Wild Roses,
And everyone awaits Spring's warmth discloses.
There are those who propose some "SUPPOSES",
As a way to compensate how our life disposes.

Memories of Bonnie will never leave me,
Her ready smiles and "thank yous" are a treasured memory.
We found blessed love and sealed it with ceremony,
Pledging our love in matrimony,
Using fond words forever recalled from love's dictionary.

Our love placed me on top of the world
As years of events arounds us swirled,
Our lives together caused love to be further grown,
But as her final day arrived, I was once again alone.

November 2018 RGP

LOVE Forever

Looking on Bonnie's diamond band on my finger anew,
Reminding me always of the love we knew
And how over our years love grew
Multiplying with four from our love of TWO.
The family expanded into a legacy steady and true.

In the wee small hours of some mornings
I awake with memories and forlornings
Our years together causes me to say, "They were adorning."
Then dawn appears and daily routines are forming.

My grateful heart recalls tender moments coming around
With Bonnie's smile lightening every moment unwound.
Because of this constant love, loneliness was banished,
Pictures remain as a tribute to her smile now vanished.

In our yard snow drifts reflect moonlite in the dark
I accept this as reflected love formed a mark on my heart
All my dreams had come true when I heard, "I LOVE YOU."
When angels ask me to recall the wonder of it all
I'll say with no delay:
"Fifty Eight years of fond memories play and stay everyday."

These are treasured memories I own without
        my spouse in the house.
They compound through tears aroused.
As summer's heat faded into fall, and Bonnie's energy diminished
There remains the sense of life together
With love and devotion now to be finished.

As many special moments were recalled together,
We laughed about how at times we undressed each other.
Those happy times are ghosts along our parade.
Miles of smiles with our love that never did fade.
As our hearts re-joined after the first Texas days
(Delayed by Roland's Korea stay)
Life flowed on and never strayed.

As our first meeting was so quickly dissected,
We were both affected
But the barrier of an ocean's miles was overcome
As letters kept our love affair from being disconnected.

03/19 RGP

My Heart's Farewell

My farewell to Bonnie's constant love
Now directs my life so amended;
With lonely days no longer by her befriended.
From our world so complete and ever sweet
Her welcoming smile was found in very meet.
Together numerous goals and tasks became complete,
While we always walked to the same heart beat.

Love arrived for me soon after she was found
Our mutual thoughts blended to form a compound,
Discovering that love for us was a total surround
Giving life and love to our family found.

My happier days have taken their leave.
Bonnie told me, "I'm sorry to leave",
So now there is a time to grieve.
Without her pleasant voice and ready smile
Echoes still resound in my heart
As her departure became final.

There are no new travel events to prepare and enjoy,
Especially she would never see a great
grandchild's fun with a toy.
Her tearful regret is a vivid memory I'll never forget.
Remembering the joy of babies welcomed in our years
Become misty reflections of love
combined, and never disappears.

Now counting life's blessings within memory's door.
Recalling love's complexity that we wore.
Woven with our enduring faith for evermore.

As my tally of love's gifts were found and never lost,
My heart senses a chilling frost.
Nothing has made the hurt go away.
(No matter what those experts say)

Listen now before your words begin,
There is a hole in my heart, I now determine
As those thoughts continue barely concealed
Memories like layers of an onion become easily revealed.

I hear "How are you?" I reply with words so few.
What can I do? How should I be now? "TELL ME!"
For I'm in a new zone entirely mine alone.
This must be measured and carefully re-defined.
Hopefully the intellect will direct the mind to unwind,
Reducing the avalanche of memories so refined.

Performing tasks that are a daily routine
Cause countless memories to appear on the scene.
I recall how we laughed often and seldom ever cried.
Now those tears denied emerge in my
presence, now to be dried.

I hear a refrain saying, "HOW SOON?"
When some grief drifts by like a grey balloon.
Some say, "Your release will be found,"
But will that require memories to be stored in a mound?

If I catalog and say, "What is critically missing?"
I reply, "shared history, her "presence," laughter and
Never forget the kissing!"

What I have derived when some moods are low,
(Seeking relief from the <u>task</u> of grief),
Now my sincere desire is to make
cheerful wishes that will endow
Our generations that follow to achieve a meld
Enjoying heights of love and devotion we found —
And so dearly held.

When these treasured memories produce warm tears,
My remembering allows love to remain alive
Through intervening years,
With no substitute possible when they reappear.

Though Bonnie is gone, the love lives on.
Remembering our love that remained so certain
Fulfilling our promises, remaining beyond eternity's curtain.

With enduring love, 03/19
Roland

Blue was always Bonnie's favorite color,
Except, she often said, "We should find a car so red."
During her lingering days I heard
"You're not going to trade off our car with the INFERNO RED?"
It sparkled in the sun (when clean)
Because burnt mica was in the paint applied.

Historically, our 1951 Ford was green.
Cream and sienna was next, then came another green,
White was repeated for the next successive two,
With the brown Le Baron found (nearly new)
Then RED prevailed for the final two.

03/19 RGP

When many beliefs confront us, so assorted
Our youth must not allow our faith deported.
Faith is needed as a lifelong anchor in our lives
OR we will drift aimlessly until we capsize.

If new paths attract with pretentious prophets in disguise
Who portray themselves so wise,
Our new-found modernity may destroy
Certainty about God's eternity.
Thus can despair define and consume our identity.

RGP 03/19

ROLAND'S NEW COLORING BOOK
On Bonnie's Birthday

Facing my new coloring book
I find it easy for me to say,
"Memories are causing my eyes
to turn from blue to grey."

And I find my heart in shades of blue
Entering each room without you.
These rooms are in shades of loneliness
So bare without your smiling presence.

There are countless memories I
wish to keep.
My only escape comes with the
onset of sleep-

Even the man in the moon now
wears a slight frown,
Reluctant to smile down
as he follows me thru town.

RGP 03/25/19

My heart knows Bonnie was from heaven sent,
I present a poem to relate my kindly lament,
Describing her presence within my heart a monument,
Unable now to deliver to her directly its sincere content.

Today my mind has wandered here and there
Revealing a treasured area in my heart now most bare,
Because her presence is gone that was so fair.
These recurring memories are forever paired
Creating tributes to the love we shared.

Time resembles ocean tides flowing with their appointed pace,
Yet in my recurring moments I find in memory's file space.
A reassurance that our hearts become anchored in a new phase
Never to be amended, altered or erased.

My darkened final days produced an emotion surge.
Phrases are now reminders prompting tears to emerge.
But those expressions will never release or erase
Vivid memories of Bonnie's frequent smiles---
Woven forever, and sealed by our love's embrace.

RGP
March 20th 2019

Nineteen Sixty Four was the year of his arrival,
In his 54 years, he became unique with no rival;
SON, BROTHER, ENGINEER, FATHER
AND SCOUT MASTER,
His achievements led to designing electric vehicles,
Thus becoming their design-master.

Those who worked with him on GM teams
Often referred to him as a friend
And leader in GM regimes;
Guiding completion of engineering dreams.

How does a dad accept a son's early departure,
-so sad-?
By recalling the joys of his presence we always had,
-(always kept alive.)
To express admiration to his heirs who survive.

Knowing so many who recall his life among us,
Always helpful when there was a question to discuss.
Our memories become echoes that now rebound,
Into scenarios never to be unwound.

Many men receive praise, but with some restraints,
As his father, I believe he is with brother saints.

With Love, from his Dad, March 20th, 2019

Brian Peaslee

Roland's New Coloring Book
On Bonnie's Birthday

Facing my new coloring book
I find it easy for me to say,
"Memories are causing my eyes
To turn from blue to grey."
And I find my heart in shades of blue
Entering each room without you.
These rooms are in shades of loneliness
So bare without your smiling presence.

There are countless memories
I wish to keep.
My only escape comes with the onset of sleep –

Even the man in the moon now
Wears a slight frown,
Reluctant to smile down
As he follows me thru town.
March 25th, 2019

POSTPONED

Bonnie was the perpetual host, never to boast,
Creating memories I treasure the most.
From the few weeks in "San Antone"
And years together are the images I own.
You owned my heart from the start.

Our life's journey came to be
A happy odyssey, molding dreams into reality.
From Alaska's frontier to Key West
We traveled with many smiles and zest,
Looking and cooking within our motorhome nest.

Til now, there never was a time for loneliness –
But that time has come with the end of your distress.
Sunrise and sunsets now seem the same
Without my loving partner to play life's game.

RGP
April 7th, 2019

The Spirit of Brian

You were with us two score and fourteen
Leaving a record of a useful life's tenure in between
Though your days here were fewer
Because there was no sarcoma cure
You bravely withstood overwhelming to endure

This example of a life well lived
Is a tribute to a faith secure
Plus HOPE and LOVE as a guide for the future.

There are profound regrets we know and sense –
Never to see grandchildren on his knee, in our present tense,
Yet beyond eternity's grey curtain
There will be a recompense certain.

April 7th, 2019

MY SIX MONTH REFLECTIONS

Bonnie always owns my haunted heart
With secure memories of her smiling face.
My heart continues to recall her gifts of grace
Always in polite taste with no pretense
Revealing always her enduring kindness.
There was no attempt to ever be clever.
Her gracious disposition revealed a quiet
charm, with every endeavor.

Now in my reflection, my desire will mention
My <u>relief</u> that Bonnie encountered no dementia
That could have dissolved our precious memories gone.

We could recall countless joys in our final days
to share,
Grateful for those years discovering love's gifts
Without compare.
We maintained our love thus to surpass
Life's future despair.

RGP
April 12th, 2019

MY EMPTY WINDOW

My gaze often scans our desks face-to-face
Recalling quick smiles while doing our paper chase,
Finishing details necessary we had to complete
So we could finish them before deadlines to meet.

My view out the window is more often now a stare,
Seeing some chores that need my care.
But Bonnie's "THANK YOU" will not be heard
When their completion has occurred.
In our kitchen no mixing sounds will be heard
With Bonnie's preparations being stirred.
Then errands can be run, not to be deferred.

My days have a sunrise and a sunset
But each of them concludes with a deficit,
Because chores completed are small contentment.
I've lost my angel to sing a song for,
Countless things make me love you more.

We fell in love completely never to pretend
With love our only guide, side-by-side to the end.
Now when morning opens my eyes,
Wishing you were there —
Another day for us to care and share.
I loved being loved by you
Realizing our countless dreams come true.
In so many ways we could have missed each other.

Yet from our diverse paths,
Cupid appeared in Texas to hover,
With aim so true we bonded together.

Now alone with memories that will not retreat
My repeated recollections, always retained,
Will remain forever sweet.

RGP
April 14th, 2019

There were times at first when my empty feelings were the worst.
Phrases were recalled, "RE-INVENT YOURSELF" OR
"GET ON WITH IT."
These ideas I found invading, although meant as useful-
(whether comments or sentiment)
I will object to them because to me it meant
Giving up memories of places found with time well-spent,
OR, if here at home with no need to roam.

My realization that Bonnie renovated and re-invented
Who I became, very happily.
She changed me for the better with loving gifts to me.

The ways Bonnie led our lives along new routes
Resulted in treasured harmonies and
worthy goals with no doubts.
So if there's mention of re-invention, I'll defy
Those thoughts that wander by.
Calmly secure I'll survive with an occasional sigh.

When all the stars stop their gleaming
Then I'll need to end my dreaming,
Easily recalling our many scenarios held so dear.
Memories will remain as if Bonnie were still here.

Though there is a space in time that leaves us apart,
Bonnie's spirit persists, haunting my heart.
With repeated pleasant thoughts that always remain.
Recalling those events together, I will gladly retain.

RGP
April 18th, 2019

Fewer Stars Are Seen

More stars have fallen since our October goodbye.
Recalling past years in quiet times I occupy,
There are moments I'm humming the wrong song,
With a sense that some words no longer belong.
Searching, but not finding, phrases to fit together
Especially when there are days of cloudy weather,
And no longer can we be here together.

My song lines seem lacking best words to choose
With the melodies trailing off as I muse.
Saying Goodbye to daily love here can make me feel
Tomorrows may emerge with less appeal.
Our love, luckily found, was bound so true
We never knew any moments of curfew.
Day-by-day we could say
Love grew even as our hands were clasped
And a final breath slipped away.
Now Bonnie's voice can only stay
To be heard on my cell phone replay.

The love in my heart became lovingly sewn,
And my life is sustained, even though now alone,
By our steadfast love we had known.

RGP
April 28th, 2019

When my present days transition into night
And with you absent from my sight,
You do become near in my mind when I think of you.
Recalling pleasant events and trips we would do.

Your love captured and owned my total heart
Sealing those bonds of love from the start.
Our love's milestones are now sublime, over time.
With love's actions always tender,
Our lives embraced a total surrender.
We had a lifetime of sharing from the time of marrying.

Though you've gone from my sight,
I recall how we would embrace
And as love's memory can revive treasured scenes
That will never be erased.

As we found your energy decreasing in slow increments
Our activities became a fraction of former enjoyments.
We then found ourselves with a mission
As we would STOP, RECALL, LOOK and LISTEN,
Knowing that tears would easily glisten.
We experienced our entry into an autumn of love's adventures,
Concluding countless pleasures we had measured.

RGP
April 28th 2019

Of all the joys that love can bring
With enduring affection and fond remembering,
My mind continues its recall of events and places,
And never erases
The special details surviving in memory's file cases.

FAITH, HOPE AND LOVE provide life's binding chain,
Words that remind, retain and always sustains
Enduring recalls hearing familiar refrains.
Thoughts revealed remain, never to wane,
Secure as a daily blessing that will surely remain.

May 1, 2019

No More

As the composer wrote, "Guess I'll
Hang My Tears Out To Dry,"
Noting that six months have gone by.
At times there has been a long, deep sigh,
With no ear to hear it coming from this guy.

Wishing Bonnie would see the flowering of our redbud tree.
A favorite perch for our frequent birds
Waiting their turn at our feeder free.
Also to see our Iowa Wild Roses soon to be lovely
Outside the window where she opened the blinds daily.

Never mind the clock that chimes
Repeating the daily appointed times
That once would be times spent together
Walking, on errands, or baking together – whatever.

We never compounded any make-believe
Because our true love we found continued to weave.
Memorable scenes that are ever pleasant to retrieve.

May 1, 2019

Seven months ago this very day
You left our family and here I stay,
Recalling your regrets of my remaining alone.
Your exit path was not by us chosen
It came upon us and became known.

Now days and nites persist, loving memories never dismissed,
From our quilt of homes, children and travel in every state
With laughter, love, good foods and good times fortunate.
With our motor home mileages on memorable excursions,
We encountered some mechanical diversions.
Returning home we prepared for future expeditions.

We can relate how our wheels had rolled
From Labrador's shore to San Diego's door.
We went coast-to-coast and into Canada to explore.
Five Hundred Thousand miles in 49 years!
Could this be a reason for timely cheers?

May 12, 2019

Here I declare Bonnie's touch is missed so much.
Moving on alone without the touch of her hand,
Recalling those passing touches (even doing dishes)
When even that moment re-affirmed love's wishes.

We recalled countless times our meeting so fortunate
To discover our "IOWA HEARTS" were sure to knit.
That month spent under a 1958 TEXAS SUN
When we could travel to find Padre Island fun,
Cruising in my fifty-two PLYMOUTH BLUE.

We found our love continued and securely grew.
In my KOREA YEAR apart, our love seemed so true.
Our lifelong devotion increased with our family new
And worthwhile mutual goals were ours to pursue.

May 13, 2019

Yearning Will Not End

Memories remain, clear and vivid with each returning.
Our wedding day, the climax of our yearning,
When love's partnership became the ultimate turning
As our lives created bonds of love enduring.

Frequently now, memories file will still urge
Evolving words that assemble and emerge
As symbols of our love's treasured role
Remaining secure, embedded in my soul.

May 15, 2019 (Roland's Birthday)

Day In, Day Out, As I go About
Completing tasks that were once done by two,
Fond memories return of Bonnie so true,
Making jokes about what some new item would do.

Our first months in the Interstater camper new
Carried Alan and Brian fenced in the upper space
Talking to us below, using the speaker tube in place,
With their "beep-beep" horn for their use.
Continuing down the road, as they slept,
We would arrive with our schedule kept.

Adding Jay and Dian with three years counting
We drove many roads over plains and mountains.
Coast-to coast and border-to-border we saw the sights
As we often camped with desserts made as camp fire pies
Seldom were there any frowns or cries.

May 15, 2019

Day's End

There was never a day our love went astray.
Our routine's included time for travel days.
Sometimes we gazed on lakes that glistened,
We listened to unfamiliar birds,
Singing songs that never had words.

No day arrived when our spirits were broken,
Togetherness was our token for fun,
Whether a rainy day or a sunny one.

"Body battles" came our way, won, until the final one.
Our goodbyes recalled events forever retained.
My love still grew as her strength did wane,
The final chapter of our love, I'll always retain
While I emerge from suspended animation.

My poems provide a slight relent
From my daily detent.
Losing my guiding star in my firmament;
When she was released from lymphoma's torment,
Was the conclusion to the inevitable event.

May 25, 2019

Today I went with every intent
To purchase Father's Day cards to be sent

Holding three cards in my hand
It dawned on me only two would be needed
Since our son, so worthy, had been interceded
That Sunday night call beginning
"Brian Speaking"
Will not be heard over my phone's speaker
(Except from my memory's refrain)
That will never grow weaker.
Tearfully
Your Dad

May 26, 2019

Gifts of Love

Bonnie's love song to me
Was not verses with words, you see –
But those acts of love so sweet
Daily in her way, always neat.

Memories of her love fill my heart
When certain small tasks I start.
I was always glad for her smile
So frequent when stopped for a while.
A "Thank you" was heard, as was her style.

Our house now so quiet and still
Needs the music I play, the hours to fill.
No one else can see the flowers bloom
Lilacs, peonies, roses, columbine and sedum.

Keeping feeders full to meet bird's needs
So they continue with a choice of syrup or seeds
Their antics at times show sensibilities
Like people, some have possessive personalities.

Time flies with memories causing me to realize
Gifts of love are still recognized without disguise.
They are evidence of love without compromise
Remaining as a gift that is a special prize.

May 27th, 2019

Printed in the United States
By Bookmasters